200 twenty-minute meals

hamlyn | all colour cookbook

200 twenty-minute meals

An Hachette UK company
www.hachette.co.uk

First published in Great Britain in 2011 by Hamlyn,
a division of Octopus Publishing Group Ltd
Endeavour House, 189 Shaftesbury Avenue
London WC2H 8JY
www.octopusbooks.co.uk

ISBN: 978 0 60062 323 6
A CIP catalogue record for this book is available
from the British Library
Printed and bound in China
1 2 3 4 5 6 7 8 9 10

Both metric and imperial measurements have been given
in all recipes. Use one set of measurements only, and not
a mixture of both.

Standard level spoon measurements are used in all recipes.
1 tablespoon = one 15 ml spoon
1 teaspoon = one 5 ml spoon

Ovens should be preheated to the specified temperature –
if using a fan-assisted oven, follow the manufacturer's
instructions for adjusting the time and the temperature.

Fresh herbs should be used unless otherwise stated.
Medium eggs should be used unless otherwise stated.

The Department of Health advises that eggs should not
be consumed raw. This book contains some dishes made
with raw or lightly cooked eggs. It is prudent for vulnerable
people such as pregnant and nursing mothers, invalids,
the elderly, babies and young children to avoid uncooked
or lightly cooked dishes made with eggs. Once prepared,
these dishes should be kept refrigerated and used promptly.

This book includes dishes made with nuts and nut
derivatives. It is advisable for those with known allergic
reactions to nuts and nut derivatives and those who may
be potentially vulnerable to these allergies to avoid dishes
made with nuts and nut oils. It is also prudent to check the
labels of pre-prepared ingredients for the possible inclusion
of nut derivatives.

contents

introduction

introduction

It is 7.30 pm, your train was delayed because it had no driver, it is getting dark outside, the washing still needs hanging up from this morning, the dishwasher needs emptying and you are starving. These are not the best circumstances in which to start cooking a meal, but let's face it, it is the reality of most Mondays, Tuesdays, Wednesdays and Thursdays. In fact, if we had the space on the cover, we might well have called this book, 'The Monday-to-Thursday Meal Book' because it is on those days that we tend to find ourselves throwing together meals in a matter of minutes. If we can't cook something tasty in 20 minutes or less, the majority of us end up pulling a ready-meal from the freezer and introducing it guiltily to the microwave, or shutting the cupboards, reaching for the phone and dialling for a takeaway meal.

In this small but useful book, we have a clear message for you. Save your money! Don't order that takeaway — in the time it would take you to heat up a ready-meal in the oven, you can make a delicious, nutritious, home-cooked supper and, more often than not, for less than it would have cost you for that ready-meal. All you need are some key store-cupboard ingredients, some vital pieces of kitchen equipment and a little bit of meal planning.

the art of meal planning

For those of us who are working all day, either looking after children in the home or in paid work out of the home, finding the time to sit down and plan our meals is difficult, to say the least. But by doing so, the next time you find yourself with a rumbling stomach, standing by an open fridge door at 7.30 pm, all you have to do is look at your meal list and find the ingredients and we promise you that 20 minutes or so later you will be sitting down and eating a tasty home-cooked supper. It couldn't be simpler. So after you have eaten tonight, instead of switching on the TV or turning on the computer, spend a few minutes going through this book. Pick out four or five meals you fancy and then turn on the computer and use it to place your internet shopping order. Keep your meal list on the fridge door and tick off the meals as you cook them. It sounds obvious, but such a small, simple task

means that you or your partner will know what food has been bought for what meal; it means less wastage of food; time is saved shopping for extra ingredients (which have been used up unknowingly on another meal); and you do not have to spend time deciding what to cook.

So which meals should you choose when planning your suppers? Firstly, be aware of your and your family's tastes and, where possible, mix up your and their favourites with some new foods. Secondly, factor in your budget. Thirdly, remember nutrition.

busy people need good nutrition

When it comes to making sure that you are getting a balanced, nutritious diet, our suggestion is that you mix up as many different types of food across the course of the week as is economical and practicable. This ensures you are getting a whole host of

nutrients and it means you won't get bored cooking the same meals all the time. It also means that, if you're cooking for a family, everyone gets to have their favourite food at least once a week.

Fruit and vegetables are hugely important to your overall health and vitality and should take up at least a third of your dinner plate. They are packed with important vitamins and minerals, such as iron, potassium, zinc and calcium, which help your mind and body to function well. When your life is busy and stressful, fruits and vegetables are especially important in your diet as they are brimming with antioxidants that help ward off illness. Remembering all the nutritional benefits of long lists of foods is practically impossible, so try and follow the simple rule that you should eat some orange and red fruits and vegetables, such as red peppers, tomatoes,

radishes, apricots, carrots, oranges and squashes, and some dark green vegetables, and herbs such as broccoli, greens, parsley and spinach, every day to benefit from their high levels of vitamins and antioxidants. Also, remember that the fresher your fruit and vegetables are, the better they are for you.

You will notice as you look through this book that many of the recipes involve steaming or stir-frying vegetables. We have included these recipes not only because these methods are time-saving and efficient, but also because heat destroys the vitamins, so keeping the cooking time to a minimum improves the levels of nutrition in your meals.

Protein should make up another third of your dinner plate. Mixing up the protein sources in your diet will ensure you benefit from a wide range of nutrients. Gone are the days when meat was heralded as the first-class protein and all other forms of protein were considered second class. These days it is recommended that, as well as some red meat and poultry, we should include a range of omega-rich fish and seafood in our diets (ideally at least twice a week) as well as plenty of nuts and seeds, some low-fat dairy products, such as cheese, milk and yogurt, some eggs and, of course, plenty of pulses. When choosing your protein, remember that weight for weight, beans contain almost as much protein as fillet steak at a fraction of the cost and with many more health benefits. Beans are rich in various health-giving minerals, and they help protect against cardio-vascular diseases, osteoporosis and various cancers. Remember, too, that they also have a low GI, which means they provide slow-release energy, an important factor for diabetics. For the sake of speed, the recipes in this book use cans of beans as opposed to dried beans which need soaking.

Complex carbohydrates should make up the remaining third of your plate and should form the basis of your diet. Complex carbohydrates are vital for fibre and to give our cells the energy they need; that's why when we get in from work at seven o'clock and haven't eaten since lunchtime, we often reach for the oat cakes or crackers for our first 'food fix' – our bodies (and brains!) know that we are

lacking glucose and need immediate energy. Complex carbohydrates do not simply refer to wholegrains, such as oats, brown rice, bread and pasta, but also to potatoes and other starchy vegetables, such as sweet potatoes, sweetcorn, and even peppers and tomatoes. Many of the recipes in this book use lots of tasty vegetables that will give you a good helping of energy and fibre.

Once you have chosen your meals, shop for the fresh ingredients and any other specific ingredients that you don't have, and why not take a look at our recommended store-cupboard ingredient list (see page 13). By keeping these foods in your kitchen all the time, you will be able to whip up an exciting meal even when you're weren't expecting to have to cook.

what ingredients should you always have in stock?

Most fresh produce, such as meat, poultry, fish, fruit and vegetables, should ideally be bought as fresh as possible and with specific meals in mind to reduce wastage. However, there are some fresh ingredients that you can always have in your fridge and freezer no matter what kind of meal you are planning to cook because they are always useful to have to hand for a wide variety of different recipes.

In the freezer, keep fresh ginger in sealed food bags and grate it straight into the pan from frozen. Fresh chillies can also be frozen in food bags and need only a few minutes on a plate defrosting before they are soft enough to chop. Fresh herbs can be stored in and frozen in case of emergencies, although be aware that they do lose some of their flavour and pungency when frozen. Most bread products, including shop-bought pizza bases, naans and pitta breads, can be kept in the freezer and cooked straight from frozen or defrosted in the microwave for a few seconds just before cooking.

In the fridge we recommend keeping a tub of crème fraîche, a small pot of double cream, a carton of UHT milk, butter, eggs, Cheddar and Parmesan cheese and a carton of natural yogurt. All these foodstuffs can be used in various recipes in this book and are bound to come in useful before they come to the end of their use-by-date.

For your kitchen cupboards, we would recommend you stock up on the following:

- Tubes or cans of tomato purée and a jar of passata (sieved tomatoes)
- Canned chopped tomatoes
- A selection of canned pulses, including chickpeas
- A selection of canned vegetables
- A jar of pitted black olives in brine
- Some canned fish – salmon or tuna
- Stock cubes, including vegetable, chicken, fish and beef or lamb
- Dried herbs, including ground cumin, ground coriander, cinnamon, Chinese five spice powder, saffron, mixed herbs, mixed spice and ground nutmeg
- Jars of ginger, lemon grass and garlic paste (incredible time-savers with very little compromise in flavour)

- Bottled oils, including olive, groundnut and sesame oils
- Dark and light soy sauce
- Sweet chilli sauce
- Worcestershire sauce
- Salt and pepper
- Vinegar, including balsamic and white wine vinegar
- Mustard seeds and a jar of French mustard
- Dried chilli flakes
- Dried pasta and noodles
- Brown and white rice (brown rice is much healthier, but be aware that it does take an extra 10 minutes to cook)
- Fish sauce
- Some sealed bags of nuts – cashews, almonds and peanuts are especially useful
- Lime leaves
- Coconut milk
- Plain and self-raising flour and cornflour

essential kitchen equipment

Making good, fast food is something you will get better at with practice, but ultimately certain items of equipment are invaluable to help you create a really tasty meal in a matter of minutes. Essential items include a mix of different-sized, good-quality saucepans complete with lids, a good-sized colander and sieve and at least two good-sized baking trays. Standard kitchen utensils include a slotted spoon, a fish slice, a potato masher, tongs, spatulas and peelers, a balloon whisk, some mixing bowls and see-through measuring jugs,

as well as some good-quality kitchen knives. You would also benefit from having:

- A food processor with various attachments, including a whisk and beater, slicer discs and a standard cutting blade. Although it is possible to chop, grate, slice, knead and mix everything by hand, a food processor does all these things very quickly and efficiently and saves you time and energy. It is a vital piece of equipment for the busy, time-pressed cook.
- A blender (otherwise known as a liquidizer), which will pulverize the ingredients and is therefore excellent for soups.
- A garlic crusher takes seconds to give a great garlic taste as opposed to minutes.
- A two- or ideally three-level steamer pan.
- A box grater is much easier and therefore quicker to use then a single-sided grater.
- A microwave for defrosting and cooking certain foodstuffs while others are being cooked on the hob.

make your kitchen space work for you

You may have all the key ingredients in your cupboards and a whole host of lovely foods in the fridge, but when you get down to the nitty-gritty of actually cooking your meal, you need to have a workspace that works for you.

Reclaim the space in your kitchen that is taken up with non-cooking items – you need every bit of space to house the equipment and utensils that you need to prepare a meal in the

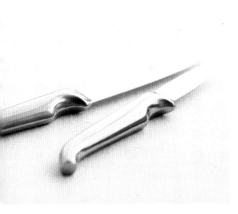

be ready to serve

Finally, when you are ready to serve your meal, be aware that needing to clear and lay the table at the last minute only adds to tension and means your culinary efforts will be left on the side going cold while you sort out the mess in the dining area. If you are eating with the family or friends, ask them to clear and lay the table while you cook — it is a good habit for children to get into, and for friends it is a small gesture of thanks for the meal you have cooked for them.

The table is set, the wine is flowing and the meal is served and sizzling on the plate. Now all there is to do is enjoy the meal you have created and revel in the fact that you have made this plate of magic in less time than it would have taken to walk to the takeaway and back. Some of the best things in life are the quickest and simplest. Savour and enjoy!

least amount of time possible. Look at your cutlery and utensils drawers and make them as easy as possible to use. Put large utensils like soup ladles, fish slices and large spoons in jugs or pots next to the cooker so you can get at them swiftly. Think about where you store your most-used kitchen equipment — ovenproof mixing dishes, graters, garlic crushers, food processors, measuring jugs and scales, not to mention your collection of sharpened knives, should be in easy-to-reach places, not stuck at the back of an over-stuffed drawer or behind a stack of heavy bowls. It may sound obvious, but you'd be surprised how habits lead us to put certain equipment in places they've been for years, but that cause us stress and waste our time when cooking. It may take an hour or so one weekend, but having a really good kitchen sort-out will really help you in your mission to make a quick, delicious meal regularly.

snacks & light bites

garlic & bean pâté

Serves **4**

Preparation time **5 minutes**

425 g (14 oz) can **flageolet beans**, drained

125 g (4 oz) **cream cheese**

2 **garlic cloves**, chopped

3 tablespoons **pesto**

2 **spring onions**, chopped

1 tablespoon **olive oil**

salt and **pepper**

To serve

cucumber sticks

4 **pitta bread**

Put the beans, cream cheese, garlic and 2 tablespoons of the pesto in a food processor or blender and blend until smooth.

Add the spring onions and salt and pepper to taste and blend for 10 seconds. Spoon into a dish and chill until required. Mix the remaining pesto with the olive oil and drizzle on top before serving with cucumber sticks and pitta bread lightly toasted and cut into thick strips.

For hummus & feta dip, put a drained 400 g (13 oz) can chickpeas, 3 tablespoons tahini paste, 3 tablespoons lemon juice, 50 ml (2 fl oz) water, ½ teaspoon ground cumin, 1 crushed garlic clove and salt and pepper in a food processor and whizz until combined. With the motor still running, pour 2 tablespoons olive oil through the feed tube in a thin, steady stream and process until smooth. Spoon into a serving dish and crumble 100 g (3½ oz) feta cheese over the top. Serve with raw vegetable sticks or toasted pitta bread.

egg pots with smoked salmon

Serves **4**
Preparation time **5 minutes**
Cooking time **10–15 minutes**

200 g (7 oz) **smoked salmon trimmings**
2 tablespoons chopped **chives**
4 **eggs**
4 tablespoons **double cream**
pepper

To serve
4 slices **bread**

Divide the smoked salmon and chives among 4 buttered ramekins. Make a small indentation in the salmon with the back of a spoon and break an egg into the hollow, sprinkle with a little pepper and spoon the cream over the top.

Put the ramekins in a roasting tin and half-fill the tin with boiling water. Bake in a preheated oven, 180°C (350°F), Gas Mark 4, for 10–15 minutes or until the eggs have just set.

Remove from the oven and leave to cool for a few minutes, then serve with toasted bread.

For egg pots with mushrooms & thyme, heat a knob of butter in a frying pan, add 1 finely chopped small onion and fry gently until softened. Add 150 g (5 oz) chopped mushrooms and the leaves from a sprig of thyme and cook until the excess liquid has evaporated. Season with salt and pepper and a few gratings of nutmeg. Divide the mixture among the 4 buttered ramekins, break an egg into each and then spoon the cream on top. Cook as above and serve with toasted bread.

peppered chicken skewers

Serves **4**

Preparation time **10 minutes**, plus marinating

Cooking time **10 minutes**

4 boneless, skinless **chicken breasts**, about 150 g (5 oz) each

2 tablespoons finely chopped **rosemary**, plus extra to garnish

2 **garlic cloves**, finely chopped

3 tablespoons **lemon juice**

2 teaspoons **mustard**

1 tablespoon **clear honey**

2 teaspoons freshly ground **black pepper**

1 tablespoon **olive oil**

pinch of **salt**

To serve
lemon wedges

Lay a chicken breast between 2 sheets of clingfilm and flatten slightly with a rolling pin or meat mallet. Repeat with the remaining chicken breasts, then cut the chicken into thick strips.

Put the chicken strips in a non-metallic bowl and add the remaining ingredients. Mix well, then cover and leave to marinate in the refrigerator for 5–10 minutes.

Thread the chicken strips on to 8 skewers and cook under a preheated medium-hot grill for 4–5 minutes on each side or until the chicken is cooked through. Garnish with rosemary, and serve immediately with lemon wedges.

For beef & sweet chilli sesame skewers, slice 750 g (1 ½ lb) trimmed rump or topside steak into long, thick strips, put in a small bowl and drizzle with olive oil and season with salt and pepper. Thread on to skewers and cook under a preheated hot grill for 1 minute on each side. Remove from the heat and coat the skewers with 2 tablespoons sweet chilli sauce and sprinkle with sesame seeds. Cook under the grill for a further minute on each side or until glazed and cooked through. Serve with a green salad.

mozzarella & tomato ciabatta

Serves **2**
Preparation time **5 minutes**
Cooking time **12 minutes**

2 **ciabatta rolls**
50 g (2 oz) **mozzarella cheese**
2 large **tomatoes**
1 large or 2 small **avocados**
1 tablespoon roughly chopped **basil**
pepper

Put the ciabatta rolls on a baking sheet and warm in a preheated oven, 180°C (350°F), Gas Mark 4, for about 10 minutes.

Meanwhile, thinly slice the mozzarella and slice the tomatoes. Halve, stone, peel and slice the avocados.

Remove the rolls from the oven and cut each roll in half. Layer the avocado, mozzarella and tomato slices on the 2 bottom halves, add the basil and sprinkle with pepper. Return the bottom halves with the filling to the oven for 2–3 minutes or until the mozzarella has melted. Put the top halves on top and serve immediately.

For pesto, mozzarella & roasted pepper ciabatta, bake and halve 2 ciabatta rolls as above. Spread 1 teaspoon pesto over the bottom halves of each ciabatta, layer with the mozzarella and a few drained roasted peppers from a jar. Omit the avocado and tomato, add the basil and season. Cook in the oven as above.

peanut, pomelo & prawn salad

Serves **4**

Preparation time **15 minutes**

Cooking time **1–2 minutes**

1 large **pomelo**

125 g (4 oz) **unsalted peanuts**, toasted and roughly chopped

175 g (6 oz) raw peeled **tiger prawns**

4 **spring onions**

6 **mint leaves**

2 tablespoons **grapefruit juice**

½ tablespoon **Thai fish sauce**

1 large **red chilli**, deseeded and finely sliced

pinch of crushed **dried chillies** or **black pepper**

pinch of grated **nutmeg**

Cut the pomelo in half and scoop out the segments and juice. Discard the pith and thick skin surrounding each segment and break the flesh into small pieces. Put the flesh into a large bowl and stir in the peanuts. Set aside to allow the flavours to blend.

Poach the prawns in a saucepan of simmering water for 1–2 minutes or until they turn pink and are cooked through. Remove with a slotted spoon and drain well.

While the prawns are cooling, finely shred the spring onions and mint leaves.

Add the prawns to the pomelo flesh with the grapefruit juice, fish sauce, spring onions and mint. Sprinkle the red chilli, crushed dried chillies or pepper and nutmeg over the salad and toss together. Serve immediately.

For pomelo & prawn salad with vermicelli noodles, put 150 g (5 oz) vermicelli noodles in a large heatproof bowl, pour over boiling water to cover and leave to stand for 5 minutes or according to the packet instructions, until tender. Meanwhile, whisk together the juice of 1 lime, 1 tablespoon sweet chilli sauce and 1 teaspoon Thai fish sauce in a bowl. Drain the noodles and pour the dressing over them. Toss well to combine. Prepare the rest of the salad as above. Toss all the ingredients together, garnish with peanuts and roughly chopped herbs and serve immediately.

chilli thai beef baguettes

Serves **4**
Preparation time **5 minutes**
Cooking time **4 minutes**

500 g (1 lb) thick **sirloin steak**, trimmed
1 tablespoon **olive oil**
4 **oval bread rolls**
4 sprigs of **coriander**
4 sprigs of **Thai** or **ordinary basil**
4 sprigs of **mint**
salt and **pepper**

Dressing
2 tablespoons **Thai fish sauce**
2 tablespoons **lime juice**
2 tablespoons **soft light brown sugar**
1 large **red chilli**, deseeded and thinly sliced

Brush the steak with the oil and season well with salt and pepper. Heat a ridged griddle pan until very hot, add the steak and cook over a high heat for 2 minutes on each side or until seared all over. The steak should be rare. Remove from the pan and leave to rest for 5 minutes, then cut into thin slices.

While the steak is resting, make the dressing. Mix together the fish sauce, lime juice and sugar in a bowl and stir in the chilli until the sugar has dissolved.

Split the rolls in half and fill with the herbs, beef slices and any juices. Pour the dressing carefully over and serve.

For Thai beef salad, cook, rest and slice the steak as above. Toss with 1 sliced Lebanese cucumber, 250 g (8 oz) halved cherry tomatoes, 100 g (3½ oz) bean sprouts and a handful each of Thai or ordinary basil, fresh coriander and mint leaves in a bowl. Mix together the juice of ½ lime, 1 teaspoon sesame oil, 1 teaspoon caster sugar, 1 teaspoon Thai fish sauce and 1 tablespoon groundnut oil in a bowl. Add to the salad, toss well until evenly coated and serve.

aromatic chicken pancakes

Serves **4**
Preparation time **10 minutes**
Cooking time **7 minutes**

4 boneless, skinless **chicken
    breasts**, about 150 g (5 oz)
    each
6 tablespoons **hoisin sauce**

To serve
12 **Chinese pancakes**
½ **cucumber**, cut into
    matchsticks
12 **spring onions**, thinly sliced
handful of **coriander leaves**
4 tablespoons **hoisin sauce**
    mixed with 3 tablespoons
    water

Lay a chicken breast between 2 sheets of clingfilm
and flatten with a rolling pin or meat mallet until it is
2.5 cm (1 inch) thick. Repeat with the remaining chicken
breasts. Transfer to a baking sheet and brush with some
of the hoisin sauce.

Cook the chicken breasts under a preheated hot grill
for 4 minutes. Turn them over, brush with the remaining
hoisin sauce and cook for a further 3 minutes or until
the chicken is cooked through.

Meanwhile, warm the pancakes in a bamboo steamer
for 3 minutes or until heated through.

Slice the chicken thinly and arrange it on a serving
plate. Serve with the pancakes, accompanied by the
cucumber, spring onions, coriander and diluted hoisin
sauce in separate bowls, so that everyone can assemble
their own pancakes.

For satay chicken pancakes, in a non-metallic
dish mix together 6 tablespoons dark soy sauce,
2 tablespoons sesame oil and 1 teaspoon Chinese
five-spice powder, add the flattened chicken breasts
and coat evenly with the marinade. Cover and leave
to marinate in the refrigerator. Put 4 tablespoons peanut
butter, 1 tablespoon dark soy sauce, ½ teaspoon cumin
powder, ½ teaspoon ground coriander, a pinch of
paprika and 8 tablespoons water in a saucepan and
mix together over a low heat. Transfer to 4 small bowls.
Cook the chicken and pancakes as above and serve
with the satay sauce.

rösti with ham & eggs

Serves **2**
Preparation time **10 minutes**
Cooking time **10–12 minutes**

500 g (1 lb) **waxy potatoes,**
  such as Desiree, peeled
25 g (1 oz) **butter**
2 **eggs**
2 slices of **smoked ham**
salt and **pepper**

To serve
tomato ketchup

Grate the potatoes using a box grater and place on a clean tea towel. Wrapping them in the towel, squeeze out all the excess moisture, transfer to a bowl and season to taste with salt and pepper.

Melt the butter in a large nonstick frying pan. Divide the potato mixture into quarters and form each into a 10 cm (4 inch) cake. Add to the pan and cook over a medium heat for 5–6 minutes on each side or until lightly golden and cooked through.

Meanwhile, poach or fry the eggs. Serve 2 röstis per person, topped with an egg, with a slice of smoked ham and some tomato ketchup, if liked.

For sweet potato rösti with egg & spinach, grate 250 g (8 oz) sweet potatoes and 250 g (8 oz) waxy potatoes as above and mix together. Make and cook the röstis as above. Serve 2 röstis per person, topped with a poached egg and a small handful of baby spinach leaves.

grilled goats' cheese with salsa

Serves **4**
Preparation time: **10 minutes**
Cooking time **3–5 minutes**

8 slices **ciabatta** or **French stick**
1 tablespoon finely chopped **rosemary**
½ teaspoon freshly ground **red** or **black pepper**
150 g (5 oz) cylindrical piece of **goats' cheese**, about 5 cm (2 inches) across
a little beaten **egg white**

Salsa
100 g (3½ oz) **piquillo peppers** from a jar, drained
1 **spring onion**, finely chopped
1 tablespoon **lime juice**
2 teaspoons **caster sugar**

Toast the ciabatta or French stick slices lightly on both sides and set aside on a serving plate.

Make the salsa by slicing the peppers as thinly as possible, then mix with the spring onion, lime juice and sugar in a bowl.

Brush a foil-lined grill pan lightly with oil. Mix together the rosemary and ground pepper on a plate.

Brush the rind of the cheese in egg white, then roll it in the rosemary and pepper mixture. Cut the cheese horizontally into 8 slices, each 1 cm (½ inch) thick, and place them on the foil.

Cook under a preheated grill until the cheese begins to bubble and turn brown. Top the ciabatta slices with a spoonful of salsa, then slide a slice of cooked cheese on top of each and serve immediately.

For grilled haloumi & olive tapenade, replace the goats' cheese with 150 g (5 oz) haloumi cheese, cut into 1 cm (½ inch) slices. Omit the rosemary and ground pepper mixture. Coat the haloumi in beaten egg white and cook as above. Put 75 g (3 oz) pitted black olives, 1 tablespoon drained capers, 1 chopped garlic clove and 2 tablespoons olive oil into a food processor or blender and whizz for a few seconds until the tapenade is a coarse texture. Spoon on to the golden haloumi, top with a handful of shredded basil leaves and serve.

black bean soup with soba

Serves **4**
Preparation time **10 minutes**
Cooking time **8 minutes**

200 g (7 oz) **dried soba noodles**
2 tablespoons **groundnut** or **vegetable oil**
1 bunch of **spring onions**, sliced
2 **garlic cloves**, roughly chopped
1 **red chilli**, deseeded and sliced
3.5 cm (1½ inch) piece of **fresh root ginger**, peeled and grated
125 ml (4 fl oz) **black bean sauce** or **black bean stir-fry sauce**
750 ml (1¼ pints) **vegetable stock**
200 g (7 oz) **pak choi** or **spring greens**, shredded
2 teaspoons **soy sauce**
1 teaspoon **caster sugar**
50 g (2 oz) **raw peanuts** (preferably unsalted)

Cook the noodles in a large saucepan of boiling water for 5 minutes or according to the packet instructions until just tender.

Meanwhile, heat the oil in a saucepan, add the spring onions and garlic and fry gently for 1 minute. Add the chilli, ginger, black bean sauce and stock and bring to the boil. Stir in the pak choi or spring greens, soy sauce, sugar and peanuts, then reduce the heat and simmer gently for 4 minutes.

Drain the noodles, rinse with fresh hot water and spoon into 4 warmed soup bowls. Ladle the soup over the top and serve immediately.

For Chinese chicken & black bean soup, cook
the noodles as above. Meanwhile, heat the oil in a saucepan, add 3 boneless, skinless chicken thighs, chopped into small chunks, and fry for 4–5 minutes or until cooked through. Add the spring onions and garlic and continue as above, replacing the vegetable stock with 750 ml (1¼ pints) chicken stock and omitting the peanuts.

seared beef & broccoli bruschetta

Serves **4**

Preparation time **5 minutes**

Cooking time **10 minutes**

375 g (12 oz) **broccoli florets**

500 g (1 lb) **sirloin steak**

75 ml (3 fl oz) **extra virgin olive oil**

4 slices of **sourdough bread**

2 **garlic cloves**, sliced

1 small **red chilli**, deseeded and finely chopped

1 tablespoon **balsamic vinegar**

125 g (4 oz) **baby rocket leaves**

salt and **pepper**

Blanch the broccoli in a saucepan of lightly salted boiling water for 2 minutes. Drain, refresh under cold running water and drain again. Pat dry on kitchen paper and set aside.

Rub the steak with 1 tablespoon of the oil and season well with salt and pepper.

Heat a ridged griddle pan over a high heat, add the steak and cook for 2 minutes on each side or until seared all over. The steak should be rare. Remove from the pan and leave to rest for 5 minutes, then cut into thick slices.

While the steak is resting, reheat the griddle pan, add the sourdough bread slices and cook for 2 minutes on each side or until lightly charred.

Heat the remaining oil in a wok or large frying pan, add the garlic and chilli and stir-fry for 1 minute. Add the broccoli and stir-fry for 1 minute. Stir in the vinegar and remove from the heat. Combine with the beef and rocket in a large bowl.

Arrange the bread on serving plates, top with the beef salad and serve.

For beef bruschetta with horseradish dressing,

prepare and cook the steak, and chargrill the sourdough bread as above. Combine the sliced beef with 125 g (4 oz) watercress leaves in a bowl. Arrange the bread on serving plates and top with the beef and watercress. Beat together 2 tablespoons soured cream, 2 teaspoons horseradish sauce, 1 teaspoon white wine vinegar and salt and pepper. Drizzle over the bruschetta and serve.

tortilla pizza with salami

Makes **2**
Preparation time **5 minutes**
Cooking time **8–10 minutes**

2 large **flour tortillas** or
  flatbreads
4 tablespoons ready-made
  tomato pasta sauce
100 g (3½ oz) **spicy salami**
  slices
150 g (5 oz) **mozzarella**
  cheese, thinly sliced
1 tablespoon **oregano** leaves,
  plus extra to garnish
salt and **pepper**

Lay the tortillas or flatbreads on 2 large baking sheets. Top each with half the pasta sauce, spreading it up to the edge. Arrange half the salami and mozzarella slices and oregano leaves over the top.

Bake in a preheated oven, 200°C (400°F), Gas Mark 6, for 8–10 minutes or until the cheese has melted and is golden. Serve garnished with extra oregano leaves.

For spicy salami, mozzarella & tomato quesadilla,

lay 1 large flour tortilla or flatbread on the work surface. Top with 2 tablespoons tomato pasta sauce, 50 g (2 oz) salami slices, 75 g (3 oz) diced mozzarella cheese and a few basil leaves. Add a second tortilla and press flat. Heat a large frying pan or ridged griddle pan until hot, add the quesadilla and cook for 2–3 minutes or until toasted. Flip over and cook on the second side. Cut into wedges to serve.

mustard rarebit

Serves **4**
Preparation time **5 minutes**
Cooking time **10 minutes**

25 g (1 oz) **butter**
4 **spring onions,** thinly sliced
250 g (8 oz) **Cheddar** or
 Red Leicester cheese,
 grated
50 ml (2 fl oz) **beer**
2 teaspoons **mustard**
4 slices of **wholemeal bread**
pepper

Heat the butter in a frying pan, add the spring onions and fry for 5 minutes or until softened.

Reduce the heat to low and stir in the cheese, beer and mustard. Season well with pepper, then stir slowly for 3–4 minutes or until the cheese has melted.

Meanwhile, toast the bread lightly on both sides and place on a grill pan. Pour the cheese mixture over the toast and cook under a preheated hot grill for 1 minute or until bubbling and golden. Serve with a salad of Little Gem lettuce, radishes and tomatoes.

For spinach & egg pick-me-ups, lightly toast the bread and set aside. Wilt 200 g (7 oz) spinach leaves in a saucepan with 3 tablespoons water, 1 crushed garlic clove and some salt and pepper. Drain well. Top the toast with the wilted spinach and 4 tablespoons grated Parmesan cheese. Poach 4 small eggs in a small saucepan of boiling water (cooking the eggs one at a time and swirling the water well before dropping the eggs in). Cook the toast under a preheated hot grill until bubbling and golden, then serve the poached eggs on top of the cheese.

pasta, noodles & rice

fusilli with parmesan & pine nuts

Serves **4**

Preparation time **5 minutes**

Cooking time **10 minutes**

300 g (10 oz) fresh or dried
  fusilli
125 g (4 oz) **pine nuts**
75 g (3 oz) **butter**
2 tablespoons **olive oil**
handful of **basil leaves**
75 g (3 oz) **Parmesan
  cheese**, grated
salt and **pepper**

Cook the pasta in a large saucepan of salted boiling water or according to the packet instructions until al dente.

Meanwhile, toast the pine nuts on a grill pan under a preheated medium grill or in a dry frying pan over a medium heat. Watch them constantly and move them around to brown evenly. Melt the butter with the oil in a small saucepan.

Drain the pasta and return to the pan. Stir in half the basil leaves so they start to wilt, add the melted butter and oil, season with salt and pepper and toss well.

Transfer to warmed serving plates, sprinkle with the pine nuts, Parmesan and the remaining basil leaves and serve immediately.

For fusilli with red onion & goats' cheese, heat the olive oil in a frying pan, add 2 finely chopped red onions and fry gently until softened. Add 2 tablespoons balsamic vinegar and reduce until syrupy. Cook the pasta as above, drain and stir in the red onion mixture. Spoon into serving bowls, crumble over 200 g (7 oz) goats' cheese and sprinkle with the basil leaves.

bacon & mushroom tagliatelle

Serves **4**

Preparation time **10 minutes**

Cooking time **10 minutes**

375 g (12 oz) dried **tagliatelle**

1 tablespoon **vegetable oil**

1 **yellow pepper**, cored,
   deseeded and chopped

2 **garlic cloves**, crushed

125 g (4 oz) **mushrooms**,
   sliced

125 g (4 oz) **rindless bacon,**
   grilled and cut into thin strips

3 tablespoons chopped
   parsley

pepper

500 g (1 lb) **fromage frais** or
   natural yogurt

25 g (1 oz) **pine nuts**, toasted
   (see page 46)

Cook the pasta in a large saucepan of salted boiling water according to the packet instructions until al dente.

Meanwhile, heat the oil in a frying pan, add the chopped yellow pepper and fry over a medium heat for 2–3 minutes. Stir in the garlic, mushrooms, bacon and parsley, season with pepper and cook for a further 3 minutes. Reduce the heat to low and stir in the fromage frais or yogurt. Stir and heat through gently.

Drain the pasta and return to the pan. Stir in the sauce, then sprinkle with the pine nuts. Serve immediately with an Italian-style salad and fresh ciabatta bread.

For tagliatelle carbonara, cook the pasta as above. Meanwhile, heat a frying pan over a medium heat and fry 6 chopped bacon rashers and 3 chopped spring onions for 3–4 minutes or until the bacon is crisp and golden. Put 4 egg yolks and 125 ml (4 fl oz) single cream in a bowl, season with salt and pepper and whisk well to combine. Drain the pasta and toss through the egg mixture, coating the pasta well, then toss with the bacon mixture and 2 tablespoons chopped parsley. Serve immediately.

noodles with prawns & pak choi

Serves **4**
Preparation time **5 minutes**
Cooking time **12 minutes**

250 g (8 oz) dried **medium egg noodles**
3 tablespoons **vegetable oil**
2 tablespoons **sesame seeds**
2.5 cm (1 inch) piece of **fresh root ginger**, peeled and finely chopped
1 **garlic clove**, crushed
20 raw peeled **king prawns**
3 tablespoons **light soy sauce**
2 tablespoons **sweet chilli sauce**
2 heads of **pak choi**, leaves separated
4 **spring onions**, finely sliced
handful of **fresh coriander leaves**, chopped
2 tablespoons **sesame oil**

Cook or soak the noodles according to the packet instructions. Drain and set aside.

Heat a large frying pan and add 2 tablespoons of the vegetable oil. When really hot, add the noodles, flattening them down so that they cover the bottom of the pan. Cook over a high heat for 3–4 minutes or until golden brown and crispy. Once they have coloured on the first side, turn the noodles over and brown on the other side. Stir in the sesame seeds.

Meanwhile, heat the remaining oil in a wok or large frying pan, add the ginger and garlic and stir-fry for 1 minute, then add the prawns and stir-fry for 2 minutes or until turning pink. Add the soy sauce and sweet chilli sauce and bring to the boil, then reduce the heat and simmer for 1–2 minutes or until the prawns are pink and firm. Finally, add the pak choi and stir until the leaves begin to wilt.

Place the noodles on a large plate and top with the prawns and pak choi. Sprinkle with the spring onions and coriander and drizzle with the sesame oil.

For prawn & lemon grass stir-fry, heat a little vegetable oil in a wok, add 2 finely chopped shallots, 2 finely chopped lemon grass stalks, 1 deseeded and finely chopped red chilli, 1 crushed garlic clove and a 1.5 cm (¾ inch) piece of fresh root ginger, peeled and finely chopped, and stir-fry for 2 minutes. Add 20 raw peeled king prawns and stir-fry until pink. Add 6 tablespoons light soy sauce, 2 tablespoons sesame oil and the juice of 1 lime. Finally, add 2 tablespoons roughly chopped fresh coriander.

fried rice with beans & tofu

Serves **4**
Preparation time **10 minutes**
Cooking time **10 minutes**

about 750 ml (1 ¼ pints)
  sunflower oil, for deep-
  frying
½ x 250 g (8 oz) block
  ready-fried **tofu**, cubed
2 **eggs**
250 g (8 oz) cold cooked **rice**
1 ½–2 tablespoons **light soy
  sauce**
2 teaspoons crushed dried
  chillies
1 teaspoon **fish sauce** or **salt**
125 g (4 oz) **green beans**,
  trimmed and finely chopped
mint leaves, to garnish

Heat the oil in a deep heatproof saucepan and deep-fry the tofu over a medium heat until golden brown on all sides. Remove from the oil with a slotted spoon, drain on kitchen paper and set aside.

Spoon 2 tablespoonfuls of the hot oil into a wok . Heat the oil until hot, then break the eggs into it, breaking the yolks and stirring them around.

Add the rice, 1 ½ tablespoons of the soy sauce, chillies, fish sauce or salt and green beans and stir-fry for 3–4 minutes. Stir in the tofu and warm through with the rice for another 2–3 minutes. Add the remaining soy sauce to taste if liked.

Transfer to a serving dish and serve immediately with mint leaves scattered on top.

For quick prawn fried rice, heat 2 tablespoons peanut oil in a wok or large frying pan over a very high heat, add 250 g (8 oz) cold cooked rice, 1 tablespoon peeled and grated fresh root ginger, 3 small deseeded and chopped red chillies, 4 sliced spring onions and 500 g (1 lb) small raw peeled prawns and cook for 5 minutes or until the prawns turn pink and are cooked through. Sprinkle with 2 tablespoons soy sauce and serve.

pesto alla genovese

Serves **4**

Preparation time **10 minutes**

Cooking time **15 minutes**

75 g (3 oz) **basil leaves**

25 g (1 oz) **pine nuts**

2 **garlic cloves**, crushed

2 tablespoons grated **Parmesan**, plus extra to serve

1 tablespoon grated **pecorino cheese**

3 tablespoons **olive oil**

250 g (8 oz) **baby new potatoes**, scrubbed and thinly sliced

400 g (13 oz) dried **trenette** or **linguine**

150 g (5 oz) **green beans**, trimmed

Grind the basil, pine nuts and garlic in a mortar with a pestle until the mixture forms a paste. Stir in the cheeses, then slowly add the oil, a little at a time, stirring continuously with a wooden spoon. Alternatively, blend the basil, pine nuts and garlic in a food processor until the mixture forms a paste. Add the cheeses and process briefly, then, with the motor still running, pour in the oil through the feed tube in a thin, steady stream.

Cook the potatoes in a large saucepan of salted boiling water for 5 minutes, then add the pasta and cook according to the packet instructions until al dente. Add the beans 5 minutes before the end of the cooking time.

Drain the pasta and vegetables, reserving 2 tablespoons of the cooking water. Return the cooked pasta and vegetables to the pan and stir in the pesto sauce, adding the reserved water to loosen the mixture. Serve immediately, with some extra grated Parmesan.

For pesto penne with sun-dried tomatoes & feta

make the pesto as above. Cook 400 g (13 oz) penne in a large saucepan of salted boiling water according to the packet instructions until al dente. Meanwhile, toast a handful of pine nuts in a frying pan until golden, being careful not to let them burn, and chop 8 sun-dried tomatoes and set aside. Drain the pasta, stir through the pesto and sun-dried tomatoes and sprinkle with the pine nuts and 100 g (3½ oz) crumbled feta. Serve immediately with a green salad.

prosciutto & porcini pappardelle

Serves 4

Preparation time **10 minutes**

Cooking time about **10 minutes**

400 g (13 oz) fresh or dried **pappardelle**

2 tablespoons **olive oil**

1 **garlic clove**, crushed

250 g (8 oz) fresh **porcini mushrooms**, sliced

250 g (8 oz) **prosciutto** slices

150 ml (¼ pint) **whipping cream**

handful of **parsley**, chopped

75 g (3 oz) **Parmesan cheese**, grated

salt and **pepper**

Cook the pasta in a large saucepan of salted boiling water according to the packet instructions until al dente.

Meanwhile, heat the oil in a large saucepan over a medium heat, add the garlic and porcini and cook, stirring frequently, for 4 minutes. Cut the prosciutto into strips, trying to keep them separate. Add to the porcini mixture with the cream and parsley and season with salt and pepper. Bring to the boil, then reduce the heat and simmer for 1 minute.

Drain the pasta, add to the sauce and toss well. Scatter with the Parmesan, toss well and serve immediately.

For spaghetti with dried porcini & pine nuts, soak 125 g (4 oz) dried porcini in enough hot water to cover them for 15 minutes to rehydrate them. Drain, reserving the water, and pat dry with kitchen paper. Cook 400 g (13 oz) dried spaghetti as above. Meanwhile, fry the porcini as above, then add the reserved soaking water to the pan and boil until the liquid has almost evaporated. Stir in the prosciutto and cream as above. Briefly toast 2 tablespoons pine nuts in a frying pan and add to the sauce. Drain the pasta, add to the sauce and toss well. Serve immediately.

tuna-layered lasagne with rocket

Serves **4**
Preparation time **10 minutes**
Cooking time **10 minutes**

8 dried **lasagne** sheets
1 tablespoon **olive oil**
1 bunch of **spring onions**,
    sliced
2 **courgettes**, diced
500 g (1 lb) **cherry tomatoes**,
    quartered
2 x 200 g (7 oz) cans **tuna** in
    water, drained
65 g (2½ oz) **wild rocket**
4 teaspoons **pesto**
pepper
basil leaves, to garnish

Cook the pasta sheets, in batches, in a large saucepan of salted boiling water according to the packet instructions until al dente. Drain and return to the pan to keep warm.

Meanwhile, heat the oil in a frying pan over a medium heat, add the spring onions and courgettes and cook, stirring, for 3 minutes. Remove the pan from the heat, add the tomatoes, tuna and rocket and gently toss everything together.

Place a little of the tuna mixture on 4 serving plates and top each with a pasta sheet. Spoon over the remaining tuna mixture, then top with the remaining pasta sheets. Season with plenty of pepper and top each with a spoonful of pesto and some basil leaves before serving.

For salmon lasagne, use 400 g (14 oz) salmon fillets. Pan-fry the fillets for 2–3 minutes on each side or until cooked through, remove the bones and skin, then flake and use in place of the tuna.

veggie carbonara

Serves **4**
Preparation time **5 minutes**
Cooking time **15 minutes**

400 g (13 oz) dried **penne**
2 tablespoons **olive oil**
2 **garlic cloves**, finely chopped
3 **courgettes**, thinly sliced
6 **spring onions**, cut into 1 cm
   (½ inch) lengths
4 **egg yolks**
100 ml (3½ fl oz) **crème
   fraîche**
75 g (3 oz) **Parmesan
   cheese**, grated, plus extra
   to serve
salt and **pepper**

Cook the pasta in a large saucepan of salted boiling water according to the packet instructions until al dente.

Heat the oil in a heavy-based frying pan over a medium-high heat, add the garlic, courgettes and spring onions and cook, stirring, for 4–5 minutes or until the courgettes are tender. Remove the pan from the heat and set aside.

Meanwhile, put the egg yolks in a bowl and season with salt and a generous grinding of pepper. Mix together with a fork.

Just before the pasta is ready, return the pan with the courgette mixture to the heat. Stir in the crème fraîche and bring to the boil.

Drain the pasta well, return to the pan and immediately stir in the egg mixture, Parmesan and the creamy courgette mixture. Stir vigorously and serve immediately with a scattering of extra grated Parmesan.

For asparagus carbonara, replace the courgettes with 250 g (8 oz) asparagus spears. Cut the spears into 2.5 cm (1 inch) lengths and cook in exactly the same way as the courgettes.

thai chicken noodle salad

Serves **4**
Preparation time **10 minutes**
Cooking time **10 minutes**

250 g (8 oz) dried **thin rice
  noodles**
6 tablespoons **Thai sweet
  chilli sauce**
2 tablespoons **Thai fish sauce**
juice of 2 **limes**
2 cooked boneless, skinless
  chicken breasts
1 **cucumber**, cut into ribbons
1 **red chilli**, deseeded and
  finely chopped
small handful of **fresh
  coriander leaves**

Put the noodles in a large heatproof bowl, pour over boiling water to cover and leave to stand for 6–8 minutes, or according to the packet instructions, until tender. Drain and rinse under cold running water.

Whisk together the sweet chilli sauce, fish sauce and lime juice in a large bowl. Shred the chicken breasts and toss with the dressing to coat.

Add the noodles, cucumber and chilli to the chicken mixture and toss gently to combine. Scatter over the coriander leaves and serve immediately.

For seafood noodle salad, cook the noodles as above. Prepare the dressing but replace the chicken with 500 g (1 lb) cooked peeled prawns and 200 g (7 oz) cooked shelled mussels. Scatter over a small handful of basil leaves instead of coriander leaves.

creamy blue cheese pasta

Serves **4**

Preparation time **10 minutes**

Cooking time **10 minutes**

375 g (12 oz) dried **pasta shells**

2 tablespoons **olive oil**

6 **spring onions**, thinly sliced

150 g (5 oz) **dolcelatte cheese**, diced

200 g (7 oz) **cream cheese**

salt and **pepper**

3 tablespoons chopped **chives**, to garnish

Cook the pasta in a large saucepan of salted boiling water according to the packet instructions until al dente.

Meanwhile, heat the olive oil in a large frying pan, add the spring onions and cook over a medium heat for 2–3 minutes. Add the cheeses and stir while they blend into a smooth sauce.

Drain the pasta and transfer to a warmed serving bowl. Stir in the sauce and season to taste with salt and pepper. Sprinkle with the chives and serve immediately.

For cheese & leek filo parcels, fry 3 thinly sliced leeks in the oil until softened and beginning to brown, then leave to cool. Mix with the cheeses as above and 3 tablespoons chopped chives. Melt 75 g (3 oz) butter in a saucepan. Put 8 sheets of filo pastry on a plate and cover with a damp tea towel. Working with 1 pastry sheet at a time, cut into 3 equal strips and brush well with melted butter. Put a teaspoon of the cheese mixture at one end of each strip. Fold one corner diagonally over to enclose and continue folding to the end of the strip to make a triangular parcel. Brush with melted butter and lay on a baking sheet. Repeat with the remaining cheese mixture and pastry to make about 24 small parcels. Bake in a preheated oven, 220°C (425°F), Gas Mark 7, for 8–10 minutes or until golden brown. Serve hot.

tagliatelle with crab sauce

Serves **4**
Preparation time **5 minutes**
Cooking time **15 minutes**

300 g (10 oz) fresh or dried
tagliatelle
2 tablespoons **olive oil**
2 **shallots**, chopped
200 g (7 oz) fresh **crab meat**
1–2 pinches of crushed dried
chillies
grated rind and juice of
1 lemon
200 ml (7 fl oz) **double cream**
handful of **chives**, snipped
salt and **pepper**
75 g (3 oz) **Parmesan**
cheese, grated, to serve

Cook the pasta in a large saucepan of boiling water or according to the packet instructions until al dente.

Heat the oil in a saucepan, add the shallots and fry gently until softened but not browned. Add the crab meat, chillies, lemon rind and juice and salt and pepper to taste.

Add the cream to the crab mixture and bring to the boil, then stir in the chives.

Drain the pasta well and return to the pan. Stir in the crab sauce, toss well and serve immediately with a bowl of grated Parmesan.

For creamy tagliatelle with crabsticks & dill sauce, cook the pasta as above. Meanwhile, add 2 large crushed garlic cloves with the shallots and fry as above. Add 150 ml (¼ pint) white wine, 4 tablespoons double cream and a handful of fresh chopped dill. Finally, mix the drained pasta and 250g (8oz) shredded crabsticks into the creamy sauce, season with salt and pepper and serve.

tuna, spinach & tomato penne

Serves **4**
Preparation time **5 minutes**
Cooking time **10 minutes**

350 g (11½ oz) dried **penne**
2 tablespoons **olive oil**, plus
    extra for drizzling
1 **onion,** finely sliced
1 **garlic clove**, crushed
500 g (1 lb) **cherry tomatoes,**
    halved
pinch of **sugar** (optional)
250 g (8 oz) **baby leaf**
    spinach
2 x 185 g (6½ oz) cans **tuna**
    steak in olive oil, drained
salt and **pepper**

Cook the pasta in a large saucepan of salted boiling water according to the packet instructions until al dente.

Meanwhile, heat the oil in a large saucepan, add the onion and fry gently until softened. Add the garlic and tomatoes and fry for a further 3–4 minutes or until the tomatoes just begin to break up. Season with salt and pepper and a little sugar if needed.

Stir in the spinach, then gently stir in the tuna, trying not to break it up too much.

Drain the pasta, add to the sauce and toss well. Drizzle a little more olive oil over the pasta before serving.

For creamy penne pasta with mussels & white wine,

cook the penne as above. Meanwhile, heat a little oil in a saucepan and add 1 finely chopped garlic clove, 150 ml (¼ pint) white wine and 1.5 kg (3 lb) scrubbed and debearded mussels to the pan (first discarding any that don't shut when tapped). Cover and cook until the mussels have opened. Discard any that remain closed. Strain the mussels through a sieve, reserving the liquid. Pour the liquid back into a clean saucepan and add 200 ml (7 fl oz) double cream. Simmer until it reaches a creamy consistency. Drain the pasta. Pick the mussels from their shells and add to the sauce along with the pasta. Season with salt and pepper.

linguine with ham & eggs

Serves **2**
Preparation time **5 minutes**
Cooking time **10 minutes**

150 g (5 oz) dried **linguine**
2 **eggs**
75 g (3 oz) thinly sliced **ham**
2 **spring onions**, thinly sliced

Mustard dressing
3 tablespoons chopped
   parsley
1 tablespoon **coarse grain
   mustard**
2 teaspoons **lemon juice**
good pinch of **caster sugar**
3 tablespoons **olive oil**
salt and **pepper**

Cook the pasta in a saucepan of salted boiling water according to the packet instructions until al dente.

Meanwhile, put the eggs in a small saucepan and just cover with cold water. Bring to the boil, then reduce to a gentle simmer and cook for 4 minutes (once the water boils the eggs will usually start to move around).

Roll up the ham and slice it as thinly as possible. Meanwhile, make the mustard dressing. Mix together the parsley, mustard, lemon juice, sugar, oil and a little salt and pepper in a bowl.

Drain the eggs, rinse in cold water, then crack the shells and peel away once cool enough to handle.

Add the spring onions to the pan of pasta 30 seconds before the end of the cooking time, then drain and return to the pan. Stir in the ham and the mustard dressing and pile on to warm serving plates. Shell and halve the eggs and serve on top.

For linguine with lemon cream, cook the pasta as above, adding 450 g (14 ½ oz) trimmed asparagus spears to the pan 3 minutes before the end of the cooking time. Meanwhile, put the grated rind of ½ lemon, 300 ml (½ pint) chicken stock and 300 ml (½ pint) crème fraîche into a saucepan and heat through gently. Add the juice of 1 lemon and 75 g (3 oz) grated Parmesan cheese and cook until the sauce has thickened. Drain the pasta and asparagus, stir in the lemon cream and some chopped parsley and season with pepper. Serve immediately.

rice noodles with lemon chicken

Serves **4**
Preparation time **10 minutes**
Cooking time **10 minutes**

4 boneless **chicken breasts**,
  skin on, each 150 g (5 oz)
juice of 2 **lemons**
4 tablespoons **sweet chilli
  sauce**
250 g (8 oz) dried **rice
  noodles**
small bunch of **parsley**,
  chopped
small bunch of **coriander**,
  chopped
½ **cucumber**, peeled into
  ribbons with a vegetable
  peeler
salt and **pepper**
finely chopped **red chilli**, to
  garnish

Lay a chicken breast between 2 sheets of clingfilm and flatten with a rolling pin or meat mallet. Repeat with the remaining chicken breasts.

Mix the chicken with half the lemon juice and the sweet chilli sauce in a large non-metallic dish and season to taste with salt and pepper.

Arrange the chicken breasts on a grill rack in a single layer. Cook under a preheated grill for 4–5 minutes on each side or until cooked through. Finish on the skin side so that it is crisp.

Meanwhile, put the noodles in a large heatproof bowl, pour over boiling water to cover and leave to stand for 10 minutes or according to the packet instructions, until tender, then drain. Return to the bowl, add the remaining lemon juice, herbs and cucumber to the noodles and toss well to mix. Season to taste with salt and pepper.

Top the noodles with the cooked chicken and serve immediately, garnished with the chopped red chilli.

For stir-fried ginger broccoli, to serve as an accompaniment, trim 500 g (1 lb) broccoli. Divide the heads into florets, then diagonally slice the stalks. Blanch the florets and stalks in a saucepan of salted boiling water for 30 seconds. Drain, refresh under cold running water and drain again thoroughly. Heat 2 tablespoons vegetable oil in a large frying pan, add 1 thinly sliced garlic clove and 2.5 cm (1 inch) piece of fresh root ginger, peeled and finely chopped, and stir-fry for a few seconds. Add the broccoli and stir-fry for 2 minutes. Add 1 teaspoon sesame oil and fry for a further 30 seconds.

speck, spinach & taleggio fusilli

Serves **4**

Preparation time **5 minutes**

Cooking time **15 minutes**

375 g (12 oz) dried **fusilli**

100 g (3½ oz) **speck** slices

150 g (5 oz) **Taleggio cheese**,
derinded and cut into small
cubes

150 ml (¼ pint) **double cream**

125 g (4 oz) **baby leaf
spinach**, roughly chopped

salt and **pepper**

grated **Parmesan cheese**, to
serve (optional)

Cook the pasta in a large saucepan of salted boiling water according to the packet instructions until al dente.

Meanwhile, cut the speck into wide strips.

Drain the pasta, return it to the pan and place over a low heat. Add the speck, Taleggio, cream and spinach and stir until most of the cheese has melted. Season with a generous grinding of pepper and serve immediately with a scattering of grated Parmesan, if liked.

For mozzarella & ham fusilli, use 150 g (5 oz) mozzarella instead of the Taleggio and replace the speck with 100 g (3½ oz) Black Forest ham. Mozzarella will give a milder flavour than Taleggio.

chinese stir-fry noodles

Serves **4**

Preparation time **10 minutes**

Cooking time **10 minutes**

150 g (5 oz) **frozen peas**

175 g (6 oz) dried **egg noodles**

2 tablespoons **vegetable oil**

1 bunch of **spring onions**, sliced

300 g (10 oz) pack mixed **stir-fry vegetables** (shredded cabbage, baby corn, bean sprouts, peppers etc.)

300 g (10 oz) **firm tofu**, cubed

150 ml (¼ pint) **hoisin sauce**

3 tablespoons **orange juice**

salt and **pepper**

Cook the peas in a saucepan of boiling water for 2 minutes. Drain well. Cook or soak the noodles according to the packet instructions.

Meanwhile, heat the oil in a wok or large frying pan. Add the spring onions and ready-prepared vegetables and stir-fry for 3–4 minutes or until softened. Add the tofu, peas, hoisin sauce and orange juice and stir for 1 minute.

Drain the noodles, add to the pan, toss everything together and season to taste with salt and pepper. Serve immediately.

For Chinese lamb & broccoli stir-fry, replace the tofu with 400 g (13 oz) lamb leg steak, fat removed and cut into 2.5 cm x 5 mm (1 x ¼ inch) strips and stir-fry for 2 minutes. Cut 200 g (7 oz) broccoli into florets and blanche for 2 minutes. Drain and add to the stir-fried vegetables. Mix with the hoisin sauce and noodles as above, omitting the orange juice.

one pot

15-minute soup

Serves **4–6**
Preparation time **10 minutes**
Cooking time about **15
minutes**

2 tablespoons **olive oil**
1 small **onion**, finely chopped
2 **garlic cloves**, finely chopped
2 thick slices of day-old **bread**,
  crusts removed, broken into
  pieces
2 **tomatoes**, roughly chopped
1 litre (1¾ pints) **vegetable
  stock**
200 g (7 oz) frozen **peas**
1 teaspoon **pimentón dulce**
  (mild paprika)
100 ml (3½ fl oz) **fino sherry**
250 g (8 oz) raw **tiger
  prawns**, peeled
1 **hard-boiled egg**, shelled
  and finely chopped
2 tablespoons finely chopped
  parsley
salt and **pepper**

Heat the oil in a saucepan, add the onion, garlic and bread and cook over a medium heat, stirring frequently, for 3–4 minutes.

Stir in the tomatoes, stock, peas, pimentón and sherry and bring to the boil. Reduce the heat and cook over a medium heat, stirring occasionally, for 3–4 minutes.

Add the prawns and cook, stirring, for 5–7 minutes or until the prawns turn pink and are cooked through. Remove the pan from the heat and season to taste with salt and pepper.

Ladle into warmed shallow bowls, scatter over the egg and parsley and serve immediately.

For Indian chicken & chickpea soup, put 400 g (13 oz) can chopped tomatoes and 400 ml (14 fl oz) water in a saucepan, stir together and warm through over a gentle heat. Meanwhile, chop 4 cooked chicken breasts into chunky pieces, removing any skin, and shred 150 g (5 oz) Savoy cabbage. Stir the chicken, cabbage, 2 teaspoons curry paste, a drained 400 g (13 oz) can chickpeas and 1 crumbled chicken or vegetable stock cube into the tomatoes. Stir well, cover and cook over a high heat for 6 minutes or until the soup is piping hot and the cabbage is just tender. Serve with warm garlic naan bread.

green bean, miso & noodle soup

Serves **2**
Preparation time **10 minutes**
Cooking time **10 minutes**

3 tablespoons **brown miso paste**
1 litre (1¾ pints) **vegetable stock**
25 g (1 oz) **fresh root ginger,** peeled and grated
2 **garlic cloves,** thinly sliced
1 small **hot red chilli,** deseeded and thinly sliced
100 g (3½ oz) **dried soba, wholemeal** or **plain noodles**
1 bunch of **spring onions,** finely shredded
100 g (3½ oz) fresh or frozen **peas**
250 g (8 oz) **runner beans,** trimmed and shredded
3 tablespoons **mirin**
1 tablespoon **sugar**
1 tablespoon **rice wine vinegar**

Blend the miso paste with a little of the stock in a saucepan to make a thick, smooth paste. Add a little more stock to thin the paste and then pour in the remainder. Add the ginger, garlic and chilli and bring almost to the boil.

Reduce the heat to a gentle simmer, add the noodles, stirring until they have softened into the stock, and cook for about 5 minutes or until the noodles are just tender.

Add the spring onions, peas, runner beans, mirin, sugar and vinegar and stir well.

Cook gently for 1–2 minutes or until the vegetables have softened. Ladle into bowls and serve immediately.

For miso soup with tofu, make dashi stock by boiling 15 g (½ oz) kombu seaweed in 1.8 litres (3 pints) water in a large saucepan, skimming any scum. Add 1½ tablespoons dried bonito flakes and simmer, uncovered, for 15 minutes. Strain the stock and return to the pan with 2 tablespoons red or white miso, stirring until dissolved. Cut 1 small leek into fine julienne strips and 125 g (4 oz) firm tofu into small squares and add to the warm soup with 1 tablespoon wakame seaweed. Garnish with chopped chives.

mushrooms à la greque

Serves **4**

Preparation time **10 minutes**, plus standing

Cooking time **10 minutes**

8 tablespoons **olive oil**

2 large **onions**, sliced

3 **garlic cloves**, finely chopped

600 g (1¼ lb) **button mushrooms**, halved

8 **plum tomatoes**, roughly chopped or 400 g (13 oz) can **chopped tomatoes**

100 g (3½ oz) **pitted black olives**

2 tablespoons **white wine vinegar**

salt and **pepper**

chopped **parsley**, to garnish

Heat 2 tablespoons of the oil in a large pan, add the onions and garlic and fry until softened and beginning to brown. Add the mushrooms and tomatoes and cook, stirring gently, for 4–5 minutes, then add the olives.

Whisk the remaining oil with the vinegar in a small bowl, season to taste with salt and pepper and drizzle over the salad.

Garnish with the chopped parsley, cover and leave to stand at room temperature for 30 minutes to allow the flavours to mingle before serving.

For mushroom pasta salad, prepare the mushroom mixture as above. Cook 200 g (7 oz) dried pennette or farfalle in a large saucepan of salted boiling water according to the packet instructions until al dente. Meanwhile, cook 125 g (4 oz) trimmed green beans in a saucepan of salted boiling water until just tender. Drain the beans, refresh under cold running water and drain again. Drain the pasta well and toss into the mushroom mixture with the beans and 2 tablespoons torn basil leaves. Serve at room temperature.

spicy fried rice with spinach

Serves **3–4**
Preparation time **10 minutes**
Cooking time **10 minutes**

4 **eggs**
2 tablespoons **sherry**
2 tablespoons **light soy sauce**
1 bunch of **spring onions**
4 tablespoons **groundnut oil**
75 g (3 oz) **unsalted cashew nuts**
1 **green pepper**, deseeded and finely chopped
½ teaspoon **Chinese five-spice powder**
250 g (8 oz) ready-cooked **long-grain rice**
150 g (5 oz) **baby leaf spinach**
100 g (3½ oz) **sprouted mung beans** or 50 g (2 oz) **pea shoots**
salt and **pepper**

Beat the eggs with the sherry and 1 tablespoon of the soy sauce in a small bowl. Cut 2 of the spring onions into 7 cm (3 inch) lengths, then cut these lengthways into fine shreds. Leave in a bowl of very cold water to curl up slightly. Finely chop the remaining spring onions, keeping the white and green parts separate.

Heat half the oil in a wok or large frying pan, add the cashew nuts and green parts of the spring onions and fry, turning in the oil, until the cashew nuts are lightly browned. Remove with a slotted spoon and drain on kitchen paper.

Add the white parts of the spring onions to the pan and stir-fry for 1 minute. Add the beaten eggs and cook, stirring continuously, until the egg begins to scramble into small pieces rather than one omelette.

Stir in the green pepper and five-spice powder with the remaining oil and cook for 1 minute, then tip in the cooked rice and spinach with the remaining soy sauce, mixing the ingredients together well until thoroughly combined and the spinach has wilted.

Return the cashew nuts and spring onions to the pan with the mung beans or pea shoots and season to taste with salt and pepper. Pile on to serving plates, scatter with the drained spring onion curls and serve with sweet chilli sauce.

For spicy fried rice with baby corn, replace the spinach with ½ small shredded Chinese cabbage and 200 g (7 oz) sliced baby corn and add to the pan with the green pepper.

chickpeas with chorizo

Serves **4**
Preparation time **10 minutes**
Cooking time about **10 minutes**

2 tablespoons **olive oil**
1 **red onion**, finely chopped
2 **garlic cloves**, crushed
200 g (7 oz) **chorizo sausage**, cut into 1 cm (½ inch) dice
2 **ripe tomatoes**, deseeded and finely chopped
3 tablespoons chopped **parsley**
2 x 400 g (13 oz) cans **chickpeas**, drained
salt and **pepper**

Heat the oil in a large nonstick frying pan, add the onion, garlic and chorizo and cook over a medium-high heat, stirring frequently, for 4–5 minutes.

Add the tomatoes, parsley and chickpeas to the pan and cook, stirring frequently, for 4–5 minutes or until heated through.

Season to taste with salt and pepper and serve immediately or leave to cool to room temperature. Serve with crusty bread.

For harissa-spiced chickpeas with haloumi & spinach, heat the oil in a large saucepan, add 2 chopped onions and the garlic, omitting the chorizo, and cook over a low heat until softened. Omit the fresh tomatoes and parsley and add 2 tablespoons harissa paste, the chickpeas and 2 x 400 g (13 oz) cans chopped tomatoes to the pan. Bring to the boil, then reduce the heat and simmer for about 5 minutes. Add 250 g (8 oz) cubed haloumi cheese and 200 g (7 oz) baby leaf spinach and cook over a low heat for a further 5 minutes. Season to taste with salt and pepper and stir in the juice of 1 lemon. Serve with grated Parmesan cheese and warm crusty bread.

tomato rice

Serves **4**

Preparation time **5 minutes**,
   plus soaking and standing

Cooking time **15 minutes**

225 g (7½ oz) **basmati rice**
25 g (1 oz) **butter**
1 small **onion**, halved and
   thinly sliced
1 **garlic clove**, crushed
1 teaspoon **cumin seeds**
4–6 black **peppercorns**
1 **clove**
1 **cinnamon stick**
50 g (2 oz) **frozen peas**
200 g (7 oz) can **chopped
   tomatoes**
2 tablespoons **tomato purée**
475 ml (16 fl oz) **boiling water**
2 tablespoons chopped **fresh
   coriander**
salt and **pepper**

Rinse the basmati rice under cold running water, put it in a bowl and cover with cold water. Soak for 15 minutes, then drain well.

Heat the butter in a large heavy-based saucepan, add the onion, garlic, cumin, peppercorns, clove and cinnamon and stir-fry for 2–3 minutes. Add the peas, tomatoes, tomato purée and drained rice and stir-fry for another 2–3 minutes.

Add the boiling water and coriander, season with salt and pepper and bring back to the boil. Cover tightly, reduce the heat to low and simmer gently for 10 minutes. Do not lift the lid because the steam is required for the cooking process.

Remove the pan from the heat and leave the rice to stand, covered and undisturbed, for 8–10 minutes. To serve, fluff up the grains of rice with a fork.

For quick paella-style rice, soak the rice as above. Stir-fry the onion and garlic as above, omitting the cumin, clove and cinnamon. Add 1 cored, deseeded and chopped yellow pepper and 150 g (5 oz) diced chorizo with the peas, tomatoes and rice, omitting the tomato purée, and stir-fry as above. Add the boiling water, 1 teaspoon saffron threads and 1 teaspoon paprika, season with salt and pepper and cook as above. Midway through the steaming process, add 200 g (7 oz) cooked frozen large prawns, then continue cooking with the lid on for 3 minutes until the prawns are piping hot. Serve as above.

spinach & gorgonzola gnocchi

Serves **3–4**

Preparation time **5 minutes**

Cooking time **10 minutes**

300 ml (½ pint) **vegetable stock**

500 g (1 lb) **potato gnocchi**

150 g (5 oz) **Gorgonzola cheese**, cut into small pieces

3 tablespoons **double cream**

plenty of freshly grated **nutmeg**

250 g (8 oz) **baby leaf spinach**

pepper

Bring the stock to the boil in a large saucepan. Tip in the gnocchi and return to the boil. Cook for 2–3 minutes or until plumped up and tender.

Stir in the cheese, cream and nutmeg and heat until the cheese melts to make a creamy sauce.

Add the spinach to the pan and cook gently for 1–2 minutes, turning the spinach with the gnocchi and sauce until wilted. Pile on to serving plates and season with plenty of pepper.

For sage & Parmesan gnocchi, cook the gnocchi in the vegetable stock as above. Meanwhile, heat 100 g (3½ oz) butter in a frying pan, add 2 crushed garlic cloves and fry over a low heat for 1 minute or until the garlic turns nut brown. Add 16 sage leaves and allow the butter to froth while the sage crisps. Drain the gnocchi, return to the pan and stir in the sage butter. Serve with grated Parmesan and a mixed green salad.

thai chicken curry

Serves **4**

Preparation time **5 minutes**

Cooking time **15 minutes**

1 tablespoon **sunflower oil**

1 tablespoon **Thai green curry paste** (see below)

6 **kaffir lime leaves**, torn

2 tablespoons **Thai fish sauce**

1 tablespoon **soft light brown sugar**

200 ml (7 fl oz) **chicken stock**

400 ml (14 fl oz) can **coconut milk**

500 g (1 lb) boneless, skinless **chicken thigh fillets**, diced

125 g (4 oz) can **bamboo shoots**, drained

125 g (4 oz) can **baby sweetcorn**, drained

large handful of **Thai basil leaves** or fresh **coriander leaves**, plus extra to garnish

1 tablespoon **lime juice**

1 **red chilli**, deseeded and sliced, to garnish

Heat the oil in a wok or large frying pan, add the curry paste and lime leaves and stir-fry over a low heat for 1–2 minutes or until fragrant.

Stir in the fish sauce, sugar, stock and coconut milk and bring to the boil, then reduce the heat and simmer gently for 5 minutes.

Add the chicken and cook for 5 minutes. Add the bamboo shoots and baby sweetcorn and cook for a further 3 minutes or until the chicken is cooked through.

Stir through the basil or coriander leaves and lime juice, then serve garnished with the extra leaves and chilli.

For homemade Thai green curry paste, put

15 small green chillies, 4 halved garlic cloves, 2 finely chopped lemon grass stalks, 2 torn Kaffir lime leaves, 2 chopped shallots, 2.5 cm (1 inch) piece of fresh root ginger, peeled and finely chopped, 2 teaspoons black peppercorns, 1 teaspoon pared lime rind, ½ teaspoon salt and 1 tablespoon groundnut oil in a food processor or blender and blend to a thick paste. Transfer to a screw-top jar. This makes about 150 ml (¼ pint) of paste, which can be stored in the refrigerator for up to 3 weeks.

cambodian fish hotpot

Serves **4**
Preparation time **10 minutes**
Cooking time **15 minutes**

1 teaspoon **sesame oil**
1 tablespoon **vegetable oil**
3 **shallots**, chopped
3 **garlic cloves**, crushed
1 **onion**, halved and sliced
600 ml (1 pint) canned
   coconut milk
3 tablespoons **rice wine**
   vinegar
1 **lemon grass stalk**, chopped
4 **kaffir lime** leaves
3–6 **red bird's eye chillies**,
   halved and seeds removed
300 ml (½ pint) **fish stock**
1 tablespoon **caster sugar**
2 **tomatoes**, quartered
2 tablespoons **fish sauce**
1 teaspoon **tomato purée**
175 g (6 oz) **live clams**,
   cleaned 375 g (12 oz) raw
   peeled
   tiger prawns
125 g (4 oz) **squid**, cleaned
   and cut into rings
400 g (13 oz) can **straw**
   mushrooms, drained
20 **holy basil leaves**, optional

Heat the sesame and vegetable oils together in a large flameproof casserole, add the shallots and garlic and fry gently for 2 minutes or until softened but not browned.

Add the onion, coconut water, rice wine vinegar, lemon grass, lime leaves, chillies, stock and sugar to the casserole and bring to the boil. Boil for 2 minutes, then reduce the heat and add the tomatoes, fish sauce and tomato purée and cook for 5 minutes.

Discard any clams that don't shut when tapped, then add them with the prawns, squid rings and mushrooms to the casserole and simmer gently for 5–6 minutes or until the prawns turn pink, the squid are cooked through and the clams have opened. Discard any clams that remain closed. Stir in the basil leaves if liked.

Serve the hotpot immediately with rice noodles.

For traditional fisherman's stew, replace the sesame and vegetable oils with olive oil and fry the garlic and shallots as above. When adding the onion, replace the coconut milk, rice wine vinegar, lemon grass, lime leaves, chillies, stock and sugar with 2 x 400 g (13 oz) cans chopped tomatoes, 1 pinch saffron threads, 300 ml (½ pint) white wine and 600 g (1¼ lb) white fish fillets, skinned and cut into bite-sized chunks. Continue as above, adding the tomatoes, fish sauce and tomato purée, then the prawns, squid rings, and mushrooms, but replace the basil leaves with chopped parsley. Serve with crusty bread instead of the noodles, dipping sauce and fresh coriander.

thai monkfish & prawn curry

Serves **4**

Preparation time **10 minutes**

Cooking time **8 minutes**

3 tablespoons **Thai green curry paste**

400 ml (14 fl oz) can **coconut milk**

1 **lemon grass stalk** (optional), halved lengthwise

2 **kaffir lime leaves** (fresh or dried, optional)

1 tablespoon **soft brown sugar**

300 g (10 oz) **monkfish** or **cod loins,** cubed

50 g (2 oz) **green beans**, trimmed

12 raw peeled **tiger prawns**

2–3 tablespoons **Thai fish sauce**

2 tablespoons fresh **lime juice**

To garnish

fresh coriander sprigs

sliced **green chillies**

Put the curry paste and coconut milk in a saucepan. Bruise the lemon grass stalk, by bashing with a rolling pin, and add it to the pan with lime leaves, if using, and sugar. Bring to the boil, then add the monkfish. Simmer gently for 2 minutes, then add the beans and cook for a further 2 minutes or until the fish is cooked through.

Stir in the prawns, fish sauce and lime juice and cook for 2–5 minutes until the prawns turn pink and are cooked through.

Transfer the curry to a warm serving dish and top with coriander sprigs and chilli slices. Serve with plain boiled rice.

For Malaysian monkfish & prawn curry, heat 2 tablespoons sunflower oil in a saucepan, add 2 thinly sliced onions and fry gently until softened. Replace the curry paste with 2 tablespoons lemon grass paste, 1 tablespoon garlic paste, 1 deseeded and diced red chilli, 4 cm (1¾ inch) piece of fresh root ginger, peeled and grated, 1 teaspoon turmeric, 1 cinnamon stick and 2 star anise and add to the onions with the coconut milk, lemon grass and lime leaves, if using, sugar and salt. Continue as above.

meaty treats

spicy pork patties

Makes **12**

Preparation time **10 minutes**, plus chilling

Cooking time **6–8 minutes**

450 g (14½ oz) **minced pork**

3 teaspoons **hot curry paste**

3 tablespoons fresh **breadcrumbs**

1 small **onion**, finely chopped

2 tablespoons **lime juice**

2 tablespoons chopped **coriander**

1 **red chilli**, deseeded and finely chopped

2 teaspoons **soft brown sugar**

sunflower oil, for frying

salt and **pepper**

To serve

150 ml (5 fl oz) **natural yogurt**

3 tablspoons chopped **fresh coriander**

Put the pork, curry paste, breadcrumbs, onion, lime juice, coriander, chilli and sugar into a large bowl and, using your hands, mix until thoroughly blended. Season with salt and pepper, cover and chill for 30 minutes or until ready to cook.

Divide the mixture into 12 portions and shape each one into a flat, round patty.

Heat the oil in a large nonstick frying pan and cook the patties over a medium heat for 3–4 minutes on each side or until cooked through. Remove with a slotted spoon and drain on kitchen paper. Mix the yogurt with the chopped coriander and serve in a small dish alongside the patties, with rice and a salad.

For herby lamb patties, put 500 g (1 lb) lean minced lamb, 3 tablespoons fresh breadcrumbs, 4 teaspoons dried mint, 4 teaspoons dried oregano, the grated rind of 1 lemon and 1 crushed garlic clove in a large bowl. Make, chill and cook the patties as above, then serve stuffed into pittas with hummus and a Greek salad.

chicken with orange & mint

Serves **4**
Preparation time **5 minutes**
Cooking time **15–20 minutes**

salt and **pepper**
4 boneless, skinless **chicken breasts**, about 200 g (7 oz) each
3 tablespoons **olive oil**
150 ml (¼ pint) freshly squeezed **orange juice**
1 small **orange**, sliced
2 tablespoons chopped **mint**
1 tablespoon **butter**

Season the chicken breasts to taste with salt and pepper. Heat the oil in a large nonstick frying pan, add the chicken breasts and cook over a medium heat, turning once, for 4–5 minutes or until golden all over.

Pour in the orange juice, add the orange slices, and bring to a gentle simmer. Cover tightly, reduce the heat to low and cook gently for 8–10 minutes or until the chicken is cooked through. Add the chopped mint and butter and stir to mix well. Cook over a high heat, stirring, for 2 minutes. Serve immediately.

For chicken with rosemary & lemon, bruise 4 sprigs of rosemary in a pestle and mortar, then chop finely. Put the grated rind and juice of 2 lemons, 3 crushed garlic cloves, 4 tablespoons olive oil and the rosemary in a non-metallic dish. Add the chicken breasts and mix to coat thoroughly. Cover and leave to marinate in the refrigerator until required. Cook the chicken breasts in a preheated hot ridged griddle pan for 5 minutes on each side or until cooked through.

lamb with tangy butter beans

Serves **2**
Preparation time **10 minutes**
Cooking time **10 minutes**

2 tablespoons finely chopped
  mint
1 tablespoon finely chopped
  thyme
1 tablespoon finely chopped
  oregano
½ tablespoon finely chopped
  rosemary
4 teaspoons **wholegrain
  mustard**
4 **lamb cutlets**, about
  125 g (4 oz) each

Tangy butter beans
2 teaspoons **vegetable oil**
1 **onion**, chopped
1 tablespoon **tomato purée**
50 ml (2 fl oz) **pineapple juice**
2 tablespoons **lemon juice**
a few drops of **Tabasco sauce**
250 g (8 oz) canned **butter
  beans**, drained
pepper

Mix together all the chopped herbs on a plate. Spread mustard on both sides of each noisette, then press into the herb mixture to coat evenly.

Make the tangy butter beans. Heat the oil in a frying pan, add the onion and fry gently for 5 minutes. Add the remaining ingredients to the pan and cook gently for 5 minutes.

Meanwhile, secure the thin end of the lamb around the base with a cocktail stick. Place on a foil-lined grill pan and cook under a preheated hot grill for 4 minutes on each side or until cooked but still slightly pink in the centre. Serve immediately, surrounded by the tangy butter beans and accompanied by mixed salad leaves, if liked.

For lamb noisettes wrapped in prosciutto, mix together 1 tablespoon finely chopped drained capers, 1 crushed garlic clove, ½ tablespoon chopped rosemary, the grated rind of ½ lemon and 1 tablespoon olive oil in a non-metallic shallow dish. Add the lamb noisettes and toss to coat in the marinade. Season well, cover and leave to marinate in the refrigerator for at least 20 minutes. Fold 4 slices of prosciutto lengthways, then wrap around the edge of each of the noisettes. Heat 1 tablespoon vegetable oil in an ovenproof frying pan and brown the prosciutto edges of the noisettes, then seal each side of the lamb briefly. Cook in a preheated oven, 200°C (400°F), Gas Mark 6, for 12–15 minutes or until cooked but still slightly pink in the centre. Remove from the oven and leave to rest. Serve with wilted spinach and crushed garlicky potatoes.

beef strips with radicchio

Serves **4**

Preparation time **5 minutes**

Cooking time **5 minutes**

3 **sirloin steaks**, about 300 g
   (10 oz) each

½ tablespoon **olive oil**

2 **garlic cloves**, finely chopped

150 g (5 oz) **radicchio**, sliced
   into 2.5 cm (1 inch) strips

salt

Trim the fat from the steaks and slice the meat into very thin strips.

Heat the oil in a heavy-based frying pan over a high heat, add the garlic and steak strips, season with salt and stir-fry for 2 minutes or until the steak strips are golden brown.

Add the radicchio and stir-fry until the leaves are just beginning to wilt. Serve immediately.

For beef & caramelized onion couscous salad,

brush 750 g (1½ lb) beef fillet with 1 tablespoon olive oil, then sprinkle well with pepper. Heat a nonstick frying pan over a medium-high heat and cook the beef for 4 minutes on each side or until seared all over but still rare inside. Remove from the pan and leave to rest. To make the onion couscous, heat 2 tablespoons olive oil in the pan over a medium heat, add 4 sliced onions and fry, stirring occasionally, for 8–10 minutes or until softened. Meanwhile, put 375 g (12 oz) couscous in a heatproof bowl and pour over 600 ml (1 pint) boiling chicken or beef stock. Cover and leave to stand for 5 minutes or according to the packet instructions, until the stock has been absorbed, then fluff up with a fork. Mix together 2 tablespoons Dijon mustard, a little olive oil, the juice of 1 lemon and salt and pepper and toss with the couscous and onions. Slice the beef and place on top of the couscous. Serve with some rocket leaves on the side.

cheat's calzone

Serves **1**
Preparation time **5 minutes**
Cooking time **5 minutes**

2 small **soft flour tortillas**
2 teaspoons **sun-dried tomato paste**
1 **tomato**, sliced
2 **bacon rashers**, grilled and chopped
4 slices **Milano salami**, cut into strips
75 g (3 oz) **mozzarella cheese**, thinly sliced
a few **basil leaves**
4–6 **baby spinach leaves**
1 tablespoon **olive oil**
salt and **pepper**

Rinse one side of each tortilla with water to soften, then spread tomato paste over the dampened side and layer the tomato, bacon, salami and mozzarella on top. Add the basil leaves and spinach and a little salt and pepper.

Fold each tortilla over the filling and press the edges together (don't worry if the edges don't stick together in places). Brush the dry outsides of the tortillas with oil and cook in a ridged grill pan or frying pan for 1–2 minutes on each side or until golden. Cut in half and serve immediately.

For cheese & ham calzone, prepare the tortillas as above and spread with 2 teaspoons pesto instead of the tomato paste. Layer 2 slices of ham, chopped, 50 g (2 oz) thinly sliced mushrooms and 75 g (3 oz) grated or sliced Cheddar cheese on top and season with salt and pepper. Fold over and cook the tortillas as above.

jerk chicken wings

Serves **4**
Preparation time **5 minutes**,
    plus marinating
Cooking time **12 minutes**

12 large **chicken wings**
2 tablespoons **olive oil**
1 tablespoon **jerk seasoning
    mix**
juice of ½ **lemon**
1 teaspoon **salt**
chopped **parsley**, to garnish
lemon wedges, to serve

Put the chicken wings in a non-metallic dish. Whisk together the oil, jerk seasoning mix, lemon juice and salt in a small bowl, pour over the wings and stir well until evenly coated. Cover and leave to marinate in the refrigerator for at least 30 minutes or overnight.

Arrange the chicken wings on a grill rack and cook under a preheated grill, basting halfway through cooking with any remaining marinade, for 6 minutes on each side or until cooked through, tender and lightly charred at the edges. Increase or reduce the temperature setting of the grill, if necessary, to make sure that the wings cook through.

Sprinkle with the chopped parsley and serve immediately with lemon wedges for squeezing over.

For jerk lamb kebabs, coat 750 g (1 ½ lb) boneless lamb, cut into bite-sized pieces, in the jerk marinade as above, leaving to marinate overnight if time allows. Thread the meat on to 8 skewers and cook under a preheated grill or over a barbecue for 6–8 minutes on each side or until cooked to your liking.

polenta with parma ham & cheese

Serves **4**
Preparation time **10 minutes**
Cooking time **15 minutes**

900 ml (1½ pints) **water**
225 g (7½ oz) **instant polenta**
250 g (8 oz) **asparagus
 spears**, trimmed
6 slices of **Parma ham**
100 g (3½ oz) **fontina
 cheese**, sliced
2 tablespoons grated
 Parmesan cheese
salt and **pepper**
basil leaves, to garnish
 (optional)

Bring the measurement water to the boil in a large heavy-based saucepan. Put the polenta in a jug and pour into the water in a slow but steady stream, stirring vigorously with a wooden spoon to prevent any lumps forming. Reduce the heat to a gentle simmer and cook, stirring continuously, for about 5 minutes or until the polenta is thick and comes away from the side of the pan. Season with salt and pepper.

Pour the polenta into a greased baking dish about 25 x 18 cm (10 x 7 inches). Blanch the asparagus in a saucepan of boiling water for 1–2 minutes or until just tender. Drain well. Top the polenta with a layer of ham, then the asparagus and lastly a layer of fontina and Parmesan.

Cook under a preheated very hot grill, about 7 cm (3 inches) from the heat, until crisp and golden. Scatter basil leaves over the top, cut into wedges and serve immediately.

For polenta with meaty mushrooms, cook the polenta and pour into a baking dish as above. Heat 2 tablespoons olive oil in a frying pan, add 300 g (10 oz) sausagemeat and fry until browned. Add 50 g (2 oz) reconstituted dried porcini mushrooms, 150 g (5 oz) thinly sliced cup mushrooms, 2 chopped garlic cloves and 2 finely chopped sprigs of rosemary. Spread the meaty mushroom mixture over the top of the polenta, cut into wedges and serve immediately.

lamb cutlets with mojo sauce

Serves **4**
Preparation time **10 minutes**
Cooking time **10 minutes**

8 small **lamb cutlets**
1 **garlic clove**, crushed
1 tablespoon chopped **thyme**
3 tablespoons **olive oil**
500 g (1 lb 2 oz) **baby new potatoes**, scrubbed and thickly sliced **salt** and **pepper**

Sauce
2 **red chillies**, deseeded and chopped
4 **garlic cloves**, roughly chopped
2 teaspoons **cumin seeds**, crushed
small handful of **fresh coriander leaves**
4 tablespoons **olive oil**
1 tablespoon **sherry vinegar**

Trim the lamb cutlets of most of the fat, scraping it away completely from the tips of the bones. Mix together the garlic, thyme, oil and a little salt and pepper in a bowl, then spread over the lamb.

Make the sauce. Put the chillies, garlic, cumin seeds, coriander and oil in a food processor or blender and blend to a thin paste. Stir in the vinegar and season with a little salt.

Cook the baby new potatoes in a saucepan of boiling, salted water for 10 minutes until tender.

Meanwhile, heat a griddle or heavy-based frying pan, add the lamb and fry for about 4 minutes on each side or until cooked but still slightly pink in the centre. Cook for longer if you prefer them cooked through.

Drain the potatoes and tip them back into the pan. Add half the sauce, toss to coat, then transfer the remaining sauce to a small dish.

Transfer the potatoes to 4 warmed plates. Place 2 lamb cutlets on top, and serve the remaining sauce separately for drizzling over the cutlets.

For lamb with spring-green sauce, prepare and cook the lamb as above. Put a handful of watercress, the juice of ½ lemon and 100 g (3½ oz) melted butter in a food processor or blender and whizz until combined. Drizzle the sauce over the cooked lamb and serve immediately.

thai red pork & bean curry

Serves **4**

Preparation time **10 minutes**

Cooking time **5 minutes**

2 tablespoons **groundnut oil**

1½ tablespoons **Thai red curry paste**

375 g (12 oz) **lean pork**, sliced into thin strips

100 g (3½ oz) **green beans**, trimmed and cut in half

2 tablespoons **Thai fish sauce**

1 teaspoon **caster sugar**

Chinese chives or regular **chives**, to garnish

Heat the oil in a wok or large frying pan over a medium heat until the oil starts to shimmer, add the curry paste and cook, stirring, until it releases its aroma.

Add the pork and beans and stir-fry for 2–3 minutes or until the meat is cooked through and the beans are just tender.

Stir in the fish sauce and sugar and serve, garnished with Chinese chives or regular chives.

For chicken green curry with sugar snap peas,

replace the red curry paste with 1½ tablespoons green curry paste (see page 94), the pork with 375 g (12 oz) sliced chicken breast and the green beans with 100 g (3½ oz) sliced sugar snap peas. Cook as above, adding a dash of lime juice before serving.

duck with honey & lime sauce

Serves **4**

Preparation time **10 minutes**

Cooking time **10 minutes**

4 **duck breasts**, about 200 g
   (7 oz) each

3 tablespoons **clear honey**

150 ml (¼ pint) **white wine**

finely grated rind of 1 **lime**

75 ml (3 fl oz) **lime juice**

100 ml (3½ fl oz) **chicken
   stock**

1 tablespoon peeled and finely
   chopped **fresh root ginger**

½ teaspoon **arrowroot**
   (optional)

1 tablespoon **water**

salt and **pepper**

Score the skin of each duck breast through to the
flesh 4 times and rub generously with salt and pepper.
Heat a heavy-based frying pan or ridged griddle pan
until hot, add the duck breasts, skin side down, and cook
for 3 minutes or until the skin is crispy. Drain off all the
fat from the pan.

Transfer the duck to a roasting tin, skin side down,
and brush with 1 tablespoon of the honey. Roast in a
preheated oven, 200°C (400°F), Gas Mark 6, for
5 minutes or until cooked but still slightly pink inside.
Remove from the oven and leave to rest for 3 minutes,
then slice diagonally.

Meanwhile, add the wine, lime rind and juice, stock,
ginger and remaining honey to the frying pan, bring
to the boil and cook for 5 minutes. If using, blend the
arrowroot with the measurement water in a cup and
add to the sauce. Return to the boil, stirring continuously,
and cook until thickened. Serve the duck with steamed
chantenay carrots, sugar snap peas and asparagus, with
the sauce drizzled over the top of the duck.

For French-style duck with orange, prepare the duck
breasts as above, then put in a hot frying pan, not a
griddle pan, and cook as above. Transfer to a roasting
tin, omit the honey and cook as above. Meanwhile,
cut the peel from 2 oranges, slice in rounds and set
aside. Put 100 ml (3½ fl oz) orange juice, 1 tablespoon
balsamic vinegar, 1 tablespoon caster sugar and
1 tablespoon cornflour mixed with a little water into
the frying pan, bring to the boil and stir until thickened,
then pour in 2 tablespoons Grand Marnier. Spoon over
the sliced duck and serve with the orange slices.

red hot hamburgers

Serves **4**

Preparation time **10 minutes**

Cooking time **8–16 minutes**

600 g (1 ¼ lb) **minced beef**

2 **garlic cloves**, crushed

1 **red onion**, finely chopped

1 **red chilli**, deseeded and
   finely chopped

1 bunch of **parsley**, chopped

1 tablespoon **Worcestershire
   sauce**

1 **egg**, beaten

4 **baps** or **wholegrain
   hamburger buns**, split

spicy salad leaves, such as
   rocket or **mizuna**

1 **beef tomato**, sliced

salt and **pepper**

Put the beef in a large bowl, add the garlic, onion, chilli, parsley, Worcestershire sauce, egg and a little salt and pepper and mix well.

Heat a ridged griddle pan until smoking hot. Divide the meat mixture into 4 and shape into burgers. Add the burgers to the pan and cook for 3 minutes on each side for rare, 5 minutes on each side for medium or 7 minutes on each side for well done. Remove from the pan, cover in kitchen foil to keep warm and leave to rest while you griddle the baps or buns.

Wash and dry the pan, then reheat, add the baps or bun halves and cook briefly on each side until lightly charred. Fill each bun with some salad leaves, tomato slices and a burger. Serve immediately with the relish of your choice.

For aromatic spiced burgers, omit the parsley and Worcestershire sauce from the hamburger mix and replace with 1 tablespoon ground coriander, 1 tablespoon ground cumin and 1 heaped teaspoon Dijon mustard.

sherried chicken stroganoff

Serves **4**
Preparation time **10 minutes**
Cooking time about **10 minutes**

25 g (1 oz) **butter**
2 tablespoons **sunflower oil**
4 boneless, skinless **chicken breasts** about 150 g (5 oz) each, cut into long, thin slices
2 **onions**, thinly sliced
1 teaspoon **paprika**
2 teaspoons **mild mustard**
6 tablespoons **dry** or **medium dry sherry**
6 tablespoons **water**
6 tablespoons **soured cream**
salt and **pepper**

Heat the butter and oil in a large frying pan, add the chicken and onions and fry over a medium heat, stirring, for 6–7 minutes or until the chicken and onions are a deep golden colour.

Stir in the paprika, then add the mustard, sherry, measurement water and salt and pepper.

Cook for 2–3 minutes or until the chicken is cooked through, then add the cream and swirl together. Spoon on to plates and serve with rice and green beans, if liked.

For chicken & fennel stroganoff, fry the sliced chicken breasts in the butter and oil as above, replacing one of the onions with 1 small, thinly sliced fennel bulb. When golden, omit the paprika and add the mustard and 6 tablespoons Pernod, instead of the sherry, flaming it with a taper. Add the measurement water and salt and pepper as above. Cook for 2–3 minutes or until the chicken is cooked through, then add 6 tablespoons crème fraîche and stir until just melted. Serve as above.

chicken wrapped in parma ham

Serves **4**

Preparation time **10 minutes**

Cooking time **10 minutes**

4 boneless, skinless **chicken breasts**, about 150 g (5 oz) each

4 slices of **Parma ham**

4 **sage leaves**

plain flour, for dusting

25 g (1 oz) **butter**

2 tablespoons **olive oil**

4 sprigs **cherry tomatoes on the vine**

150 ml (½ pint) **dry white wine**

salt and **pepper**

Lay each chicken breast between 2 sheets of clingfilm and flatten with a rolling pin or meat mallet until wafer thin. Season with salt and pepper.

Lay a slice of Parma ham on each chicken breast, followed by a sage leaf. Secure the sage and ham in position with a cocktail stick, then lightly dust both sides of the chicken with flour. Season again with salt and pepper.

Heat the butter and oil in a large frying pan over a high heat, add the chicken and cook for 4–5 minutes on each side or until the juices run clear when pierced with a knife. Add the tomatoes and wine to the pan and bubble until the wine has thickened and reduced by about half. Serve immediately, accompanied by a green salad.

For veal escalopes with rosemary & pancetta,

take 4 veal escalopes, about 150 g (5 oz) each, and flatten as above. Top each flattened escalope with a scattering of rosemary leaves, then wrap each in a slice of pancetta, instead of the Parma ham, omitting the sage. Dust with flour, season with salt and pepper and cook as above.

taverna-style grilled lamb with feta

Serves **4**
Preparation time **8 minutes**
Cooking time **6–8 minutes**

500 g (1 lb) leg or shoulder of
  lamb, diced

Marinade
2 tablespoons chopped
  oregano
1 tablespoon chopped
  rosemary
grated rind of **1 lemon**
2 tablespoons olive oil
salt and **pepper**

Feta salad
200 g (7 oz) **feta cheese**,
  sliced
1 tablespoon chopped
  oregano
2 tablespoons chopped
  parsley
grated rind and juice of
  1 lemon
½ small **red onion**, finely sliced
3 tablespoons **olive oil**

Mix together the marinade ingredients in a non-metallic bowl, then add the lamb and mix to coat thoroughly. Thread the meat on to 4 skewers.

Arrange the sliced feta on a large serving dish and sprinkle over the herbs, lemon rind and sliced onion. Drizzle over the lemon juice and oil and season with salt and pepper.

Cook the lamb skewers under a preheated hot grill or in a griddle pan, turning frequently, for 6–8 minutes or until browned and almost cooked through. Remove from the grill or pan and leave to rest for 1–2 minutes.

Serve the lamb, with any pan juices poured over, with the salad and accompanied with plenty of crusty bread, if liked.

For pork with red cabbage, replace the lamb with 500 g (1 lb) lean, boneless pork, diced. Marinate and cook the pork as above. Replace the feta with 250 g (8 oz) finely chopped red cabbage. Omit the oregano and replace the lemon with an orange. Mix the salad ingredients together and leave to marinate for 5 minutes before serving.

chicken livers with marsala & raisins

Serves **4**
Preparation time **10 minutes**
Cooking time about **10 minutes**

400 g (13 oz) fresh **chicken livers**
25 g (1 oz) **butter**
2 tablespoons **olive oil**
25 g (1 oz) **raisins**
6 tablespoons **Marsala**
squeeze of **lemon juice**
salt and **pepper**
plenty of chopped **chives**, to garnish

Rinse the livers and pat them dry on kitchen paper. Cut each into about 4 pieces, cutting out and discarding any white parts. Season with salt and pepper.

Heat the butter and oil in a frying pan. When it is very hot, add the livers and fry them quickly, turning them so they brown evenly, for 5 minutes or until golden. If you prefer the livers well done, fry them for a further couple of minutes. Add the raisins and fry for 1 minute. Remove the livers and raisins with a slotted spoon and keep warm.

Add the Marsala to the pan and bring to the boil. Cook for a couple of minutes until syrupy, then stir in the lemon juice. Pour the sauce over the livers and serve scattered with chives.

For rustic chicken livers, heat the butter in a frying pan, add 1 thinly sliced onion and 150 g (5 oz) chopped bacon and fry for 5–6 minutes or until the bacon is crisping up and the onion has softened. Add the prepared chicken livers and cook as above, omitting the raisins. Remove with a slotted spoon and keep warm. Add 25 g (1 oz) plain flour to the pan juices, then slowly stir in 6 tablespoons red wine to make a smooth sauce. Pour over the livers, bacon and onion and serve immediately.

indonesian beef strips

Serves **4**

Preparation time **5 minutes**

Cooking time **8 minutes**

1 **onion**, roughly chopped

2 **garlic cloves**, peeled

2.5 cm (1 inch) piece of fresh
root ginger, peeled and
sliced

1 **red chilli**, deseeded

2 tablespoons **dried shrimp**

3 tablespoons **groundnut oil**

500 g (1 lb) **lean beef,** cut
into thin strips

1 tablespoon **tamarind paste**

2 tablespoons **dark soy sauce**

4 tablespoons **water**

1 teaspoon **demerara
sugar**

small handful of **mint leaves,**
shredded, plus extra whole
ones to garnish

salt and **pepper**

1 tablespoon **snipped chives,**
to garnish

Put the onion, garlic, ginger, chilli and dried shrimp in
a food processor or blender and blend until it forms a
smooth paste.

Heat the oil in a wok or large frying pan over a medium
heat, add the paste and cook, stirring continuously, for
about 2 minutes or until the oil separates from the other
ingredients.

Add the beef and stir-fry until the meat turns opaque,
then add the tamarind paste, soy sauce and the water.
Simmer, uncovered, for 2–3 minutes or until most of the
liquid has evaporated and the meat is tender.

Stir in the sugar and shredded mint leaves, season to
taste with salt and pepper and garnish with chives and
a few whole mint leaves. Serve with a vegetable dish
and rice, if liked.

For pork with yellow peppers & mushrooms,

replace the beef with 500 g (1 lb) lean pork, cut into
thin strips, and add 1 yellow pepper, cored, deseeded
and cut into thin strips, and 75g (3 oz) halved chestnut
mushrooms. Follow the recipe as above, adding the
additional vegetables to the wok or pan with the meat.

griddled salsa chicken

Serves 4
Preparation time **10 minutes**
Cooking time **6 minutes**

4 boneless **chicken breasts**,
   skin on, about 150 g (5 oz)
   each
3 tablespoons **olive oil**
salt and **pepper**

Salsa
1 **red onion**, finely chopped
2 **tomatoes**, deseeded and
   diced
1 **cucumber**, finely diced
1 **red chilli**, deseeded and
   finely chopped
small handful of **fresh
   coriander leaves**, chopped
juice of 1 **lime**

Remove the skin from the chicken breasts. Using kitchen scissors, cut each breast in half lengthways but without cutting the whole way through. Open each breast out flat. Brush with the oil and season well with salt and pepper.

Heat a ridged griddle pan until very hot, add the chicken breasts and cook for 3 minutes on each side or until cooked through and grill-marked.

Meanwhile, make the salsa. Mix together the onion, tomatoes, cucumber, red chilli, coriander and lime juice. Season well with salt and pepper.

Serve the chicken hot with the spicy salsa spooned over and around.

For griddled tuna with pineapple salsa, prepare and cook 4 thick fresh tuna steaks, about 175 g (6 oz) each, as for the butterflied chicken breasts above. Meanwhile, in a bowl, mix together 6 tablespoons roughly diced drained canned pineapple, 1 finely chopped red onion, 1 tablespoon peeled and finely chopped fresh root ginger, 1 deseeded and finely chopped red chilli, the grated rind and juice of 1 lime, 2 teaspoons clear honey and salt and pepper to taste. Serve the pineapple salsa with the griddled tuna.

devilled fillet steaks

Serves **4**
Preparation time **10 minutes**
Cooking time **10 minutes**

2 tablespoons **olive oil**
4 **fillet steaks**, about 175 g
  (6 oz) each
2 tablespoons **balsamic
  vinegar**
75 ml (3 fl oz) **full-bodied red
  wine**
4 tablespoons **beef stock**
2 **garlic cloves**, chopped
1 teaspoon crushed **fennel
  seeds**
1 tablespoon **sun-dried
  tomato purée**
½ teaspoon crushed **dried
  chillies**
salt and **pepper**
chopped **flat-leaf parsely**, to
  garnish

Heat the oil in a nonstick frying pan until smoking hot, add the steaks and cook over a very high heat for about 2 minutes on each side, if you want your steaks to be medium rare. Remove from the pan, season with salt and pepper and keep warm.

Pour the vinegar, wine and stock into the pan and boil for 30 seconds, scraping any sediment from the base of the pan. Add the garlic and fennel seeds, then whisk in the sun-dried tomato purée and crushed chillies. Bring the sauce to the boil, then boil fast to reduce down until syrupy.

Transfer the steaks to warmed serving plates, pouring any collected meat juices into the sauce. Return the sauce to the boil, then season with salt and pepper.

Slice the steaks before serving, if you wish. Pour the sauce over the steaks and serve immediately, garnished with chopped parsley.

For devilled chicken breasts, heat the oil as above and cook 4 boneless, skinless chicken breasts for 5 minutes on each side or until cooked through. Leaving the chicken in the pan, follow the recipe above, replacing the beef stock with 4 tablespoons chicken stock and using ½ teaspoon dried oregano instead of the fennel seeds.

fish & seafood

galician-style monkfish

Serves **4**

Preparation time **10 minutes**

Cooking time **10 minutes**

15 whole **blanched almonds**

800 g (1 lb 10 oz) **monkfish fillet**, skinned

1 **onion**, thinly sliced

olive oil, for drizzling

3 **garlic cloves**, crushed

large pinch of **saffron threads**, crushed

1 tablespoon finely chopped **parsley**

250 g (8 oz) fresh or frozen **peas**

salt and **pepper**

Roast the almonds in a dry frying pan over a medium heat for a few minutes until toasted.

Cut the monkfish into 8 evenly sized pieces. Spread the onion over the base of a medium-sized flameproof casserole and arrange the monkfish over the top. Season to taste with salt and pepper and drizzle over a little oil. Cover tightly and cook over a medium heat for 5–6 minutes.

Meanwhile, in a food processor add the almonds, garlic, saffron and parsley, and blitz until finely chopped. Add 2–3 tablespoons water and blitz again to make a coarse paste.

Remove the lid from the casserole, spread the almond mixture over the top of the fish and add the peas. Re-cover and cook for a further 4–5 minutes or until the fish is cooked through. Serve immediately.

For monkfish wrapped in Parma ham, prepare the monkfish as above and wrap each piece in a slice of Parma ham, then season with pepper. Heat 1 tablespoon olive oil in a frying pan, add the monkfish and fry for 2–3 minutes on each side or until browned. Place in a roasting tin and cook in a preheated oven, 220°C (425°F), Gas Mark 7, for 8 minutes or until cooked through. Remove from the oven and leave to rest for 5 minutes. Heat 1 tablespoon olive oil in the pan, add 1 chopped onion and 2 crushed garlic cloves and fry gently until softened. Add 500 g (1 lb) cherry tomatoes and a handful of chopped basil and stir together well. Serve the monkfish on a bed of wilted spinach leaves with the tomatoes.

lime & coconut squid

Serves **2**
Preparation time **15 minutes**
Cooking time **5 minutes**

10–12 prepared **baby
 squid**, about 375 g (12 oz)
 including tentacles, cleaned
4 **limes**, halved

Dressing
2 **red chillies**, deseeded and
 finely chopped
finely grated rind and juice of
 2 **limes**
2.5 cm (1 inch) piece of **fresh
 root ginger**, peeled and
 grated
100 g (3½ oz) freshly grated
 coconut
4 tablespoons **groundnut oil**
1–2 tablespoons **chilli oil**
1 tablespoon **white wine
 vinegar**

Cut down the side of each squid so that they can be
laid flat on a chopping board. Using a sharp knife, lightly
score the inside flesh in a crisscross pattern.

Mix all the dressing ingredients together in a bowl. Toss
the squid in half the dressing until thoroughly coated.

Heat a ridged griddle pan until smoking hot, add the
limes, cut side down, and cook for 2 minutes or until
well charred. Remove from the pan and set aside.
Keeping the griddle pan very hot, add the squid pieces
and cook for 1 minute. Turn them over and cook for
a further minute or until they turn white, lose their
transparency and are charred.

Transfer the squid to a chopping board and cut into
strips. Drizzle with the remaining dressing and serve
immediately with the charred limes and a salad of mixed
green leaves.

For lemon & garlic squid, remove the tentacles from
the prepared squid and slice the bodies into rings.
Place in a non-metallic dish with the juice of 1 lemon
and leave to marinate for 5 minutes. Heat 75 ml
(3 fl oz) olive oil in a large frying pan and add 3 chopped
garlic cloves and the grated rind of 1 lemon. When the
oil is very hot, add the squid and cook over a high heat
for 1–2 minutes or until it turns white and loses its
transparency. Season with salt and pepper and serve
sprinkled with parsley and lemon wedges.

sugar & spice salmon

Serves **4**

Preparation time **5 minutes**

Cooking time **10 minutes**

4 **salmon fillets**, about
200 g (7 oz) each

3 tablespoons **light
muscovado sugar**

2 **garlic cloves**, crushed

1 teaspoon **cumin seeds**,
crushed

1 teaspoon smoked or ordinary
paprika

1 tablespoon **white wine
vinegar**

3 tablespoons **groundnut oil**

salt and **pepper**

½ teaspoon **cumin seeds**,
crushed

2 **courgettes**, sliced into thin
ribbons

lemon or **lime slices**, to serve

Put the salmon fillets in a lightly oiled roasting tin.
Mix together the sugar, garlic, cumin seeds, paprika,
vinegar and a little salt in a bowl, then spread the
mixture all over the fish so that it is thinly coated.
Drizzle with 1 tablespoon of oil.

Bake in a preheated oven, 220°C (425°F), Gas Mark 7,
for 10 minutes or until the fish is cooked through.

Heat the remaining oil in a large frying pan, add the
crushed cumin seeds and fry for 10 seconds. Add the
courgette ribbons, season with salt and pepper and
stir-fry for 2–3 minutes until just softened.

Transfer to warm serving plates and serve the salmon
on top, garnished with lemon or lime wedges.

For salmon with pesto crust, put the salmon in
a lightly oiled roasting tin, season with pepper
and add a squeeze of lemon juice. Mix together
4 tablespoons pesto and 2 handfuls of fresh white
breadcrumbs in a bowl, then spread on top of the
salmon. Grate Parmesan cheese over the top and
drizzle with olive oil. Bake as above and serve with
green beans and new potatoes.

skate with balsamic butter

Serves **2**
Preparation time **5 minutes**
Cooking time **15 minutes**

2 teaspoons **plain flour**
2 **skate wings**, about
   200 g (7 oz) each
50 g (2 oz) **butter**
3 tablespoons **balsamic
   vinegar**
1 tablespoon **capers**, drained
salt and **pepper**

Mix the flour with a little salt and pepper and use it to dust the skate wings.

Heat a knob of the butter in a large frying pan, add the skate and fry gently for about 5 minutes on each side or until cooked through. Remove with a slotted spoon and keep warm on serving plates.

Add the remaining butter, balsamic vinegar and capers to the pan and cook over a medium heat, whisking until bubbling and syrupy. Season to taste with salt and pepper, then pour over the skate. Serve immediately with boiled baby new potatoes tossed in chopped parsley and a side salad.

For skate wings with lime & coriander tartare sauce, first make the tartare sauce. Break 1 egg into the bowl of a food processor, add ½ teaspoon sea salt, 1 peeled garlic clove and ½ teaspoon mustard powder, then switch the motor on and pour 175 ml (6 fl oz) olive oil through the feed tube in a thin, steady stream. When all the oil has been added and the sauce has thickened, add 1 dessertspoon lime juice, 1 tablespoon drained capers, 4 cornichons, 1 tablespoon chopped coriander and some pepper. Switch on the pulse button and pulse until the ingredients are chopped. Cook the skate in a knob of butter as above and serve with the sauce.

clams with tomatoes

Serves **4**
Preparation time **10 minutes**
Cooking time **10 minutes**

2 tablespoons **olive oil**
3 **garlic cloves**, finely chopped
2 ri**pe tomatoes**, finely
  chopped
1 kg (2 lb) live **clams**, cleaned
125 ml (4 fl oz) **Manzanilla
  sherry**
4 tablespoons finely chopped
  parsley
salt and **pepper**

Heat the oil in a large frying pan, add the garlic and tomatoes and cook over a medium heat, stirring, for 3–4 minutes.

Discard any clams that won't shut when tapped, then add them to the pan with the sherry and parsley. Season to taste with salt and pepper, then cover tightly and cook over a high heat, shaking the pan vigorously several times, for 4–5 minutes or until the clams have opened. Discard any that remain closed.

Serve the clams immediately in their cooking liquid or leave to cool to room temperature.

For linguine alle vongole, prepare the clams as above. Cook 400 g (13 oz) dried linguine in a large saucepan of salted boiling water according to the packet instructions until al dente. Meanwhile, heat 1 tablespoon olive oil in a large saucepan, add 1 chopped garlic clove and 1 crumbled dried chilli and cook until softened. Add the clams and increase the heat to high, then add 100 ml (3½ fl oz) vermouth and cover tightly. Cook as above, discarding any clams that remain closed. Drain the pasta, add to the clams and toss well, stir through some chopped parsley and serve immediately.

tuna steaks with green salsa

Serves **4**
Preparation time **15 minutes**,
   plus marinating
Cooking time **2–4 minutes**

2 tablespoons **olive oil**
grated rind of 1 **lemon**
2 teaspoons chopped **parsley**
½ teaspoon crushed
   coriander seeds
4 fresh **tuna steaks**, about
   150 g (5 oz) each
salt and **pepper**

Salsa
2 tablespoons **capers**, drained
   and chopped
2 tablespoons chopped
   cornichons
1 tablespoon finely chopped
   parsley
2 teaspoons chopped **chives**
2 teaspoons finely chopped
   chervil
30 g (1½ oz) pitted **green
   olives**, chopped
1 **shallot,** finely chopped
   (optional)
2 tablespoons **lemon juice**
2 tablespoons **olive oil**

Mix together the oil, lemon rind, parsley and coriander seeds with plenty of pepper in a non-metallic dish. Add the tuna steaks and coat evenly with the mixture. Leave to marinate while you make the salsa.

Make the salsa by mixing together all the ingredients in a bowl. Season to taste with salt and pepper and set aside for the flavours to infuse.

Heat a ridged griddle pan or frying pan until hot, add the tuna steaks and cook for 1–2 minutes on each side or until seared all over. The tuna should be well seared but rare. Remove from the pan and leave to rest for 2–3 minutes.

Serve the tuna steaks with a spoonful of salsa, a dressed salad and plenty of fresh crusty bread.

For yellow pepper & mustard salsa, to serve as an alternative accompaniment, mix together in a bowl 2 cored, deseeded and finely chopped yellow peppers, 1 tablespoon Dijon mustard, 2 tablespoons each finely chopped chives, parsley and dill, 1 teaspoon sugar, 1 tablespoon cider vinegar and 2 tablespoons olive oil.

scallops with citrus dressing

Serves **4**

Preparation time **10 minutes**

Cooking time **10 minutes**

16 large raw **prawns**

24 **fresh scallops**, roe removed

1 large, ripe but firm **mango**, peeled, stoned and cut into chunks

2 tablespoons **oil**, for frying

125 g (4 oz) **mixed salad leaves**

Citrus dressing

juice of ½ **pink grapefruit**

finely grated rind and juice of 1 **lime**

1 teaspoon **clear honey**

1 tablespoon **raspberry vinegar**

75 ml (3 fl oz) **lemon oil**

Make the citrus dressing by mixing together all the ingredients in a small bowl.

Poach the prawns in a saucepan of simmering water for 2 minutes or until they turn pink. Drain well.

Put the scallops, mango and prawns in a bowl and pour over 3 tablespoons of the dressing. Mix well to coat, then thread them alternately on to 8 skewers.

Heat the oil in a large frying pan over a medium heat, add the skewers and fry, turning and basting occasionally, for about 5–7 minutes or until golden brown and cooked through.

Arrange the skewers on plates with the salad leaves and serve with the remaining dressing.

For haloumi & mango kebabs with citrus dressing, replace the scallops and prawns with 450–500 g (14½ oz–1 lb) haloumi cheese, cut into cubes. Coat with the dressing, thread on to skewers with the mango and fry as above. Alternatively, cook over a barbecue for about 5–7 minutes or until slightly charred.

griddled red snapper with spinach

Serves **4**

Preparation time **5 minutes**

Cooking time **8 minutes**

4 **red snapper fillets**, about
175 g (6 oz) each

250 g (8 oz) **baby leaf
spinach**

1 teaspoon **pumpkin seeds**

1 teaspoon **sunflower seeds**

2 teaspoons **olive oil**

1 bunch of **spring onions**,
shredded, to garnish

Heat a griddle pan over a medium heat, add the snapper fillets and cook for 4 minutes on each side or until cooked through and the fish flakes easily when pressed with a fork.

Meanwhile, steam the spinach until just tender. Drain well, then mix the pumpkin seeds, sunflower seeds and oil with the spinach in a bowl. Serve immediately with the snapper fillets on top, garnished with the shredded spring onions.

For griddled red snapper with couscous, put 250 g (8 oz) couscous in a heatproof bowl and pour over 300 ml (½ pint) boiling vegetable stock. Cover and leave to stand for 8 minutes or according to the packet instructions, until the stock has been absorbed, then fluff up with a fork. Drain 250 g (8 oz) mixed roasted peppers in oil (no need to chop them up) and mix with 1 tablespoon ground cumin, 1 tablespoon ground coriander and 1 tablespoon olive oil into the couscous. Cook the snapper fillets as above and serve on a bed of couscous, sprinkled with the shredded spring onions.

prawns with garlicky beans

Serves **4**
Preparation time **10 minutes**
Cooking time **10 minutes**

4 tablespoons **olive oil**
1 large **onion**, finely chopped
3 **garlic cloves**, crushed
2 x 400 g (13 oz) cans
   cannellini, haricot or **butter
   beans**, drained
100 ml (3½ fl oz) **vegetable** or
   fish stock
400 g (13 oz) **raw peeled
   prawns**
½ teaspoon **mild sweet
   paprika**
2 tablespoons **sun-dried
   tomato paste**
1 tablespoon chopped
   oregano
2 teaspoons **clear honey**
pepper

Heat 2 tablespoons of the oil in a saucepan, add the onion and fry gently for 5 minutes. Add the garlic and fry for a further minute.

Remove the pan from the heat. Tip in the beans and use a potato masher to crush them. Add the stock and plenty of pepper and set aside.

Dust the prawns with the paprika and a little salt. Heat the remaining oil in a frying pan, add the prawns and fry for 5–6 minutes, turning once or twice during cooking, until they turn pink and are cooked through. Stir in the tomato paste, oregano, honey and 2 tablespoons water and cook for 2–3 minutes or until it begins to bubble.

Meanwhile, reheat the pan with the beans until piping hot. Spoon the bean mixture into small dishes, pile the prawns on top and pour over the cooking juices.

For blackened cod with garlicky beans, prepare and cook the beans as above. Spread one side of each of 4 x 175g (6oz) cod fillets with 1 heaped teaspoon of ready-made black olive tapenade. Heat 2 tablespoons olive oil in a griddle pan over a medium heat, add the fish and cook for about 5 minutes on each side or until cooked through. Serve on a bed of crushed beans, sprinkle with chopped black olives and parsley.

pasta crab & rocket salad

Serves **1**
Preparation time **5 minutes**,
  plus cooling
Cooking time **10 minutes**

50 g (2 oz) dried **pasta**, such
  as rigatoni
grated rind and juice of ½ **lime**
2 tablespoons **crème fraîche**
85 g (3¼ oz) can **crab meat,**
  drained
8 **cherry tomatoes**, halved
handful of **rocket leaves**

Cook the pasta in a saucepan of boiling water
according to the packet instructions until al dente.
Drain well and leave to cool.

Mix together the lime rind and juice, crème fraîche
and crab meat in a large bowl. Add the cooled pasta
and mix again.

Add the tomatoes and rocket leaves to the bowl, toss
everything together and serve.

For pasta salad with tuna & chilli, cook the pasta
as above. Drain a 140 g (4½ oz) can of tuna and mix
through the cooled pasta. Add 1 deseeded and finely
chopped red chilli, the grated rind and juice of 1 lemon,
2 tablespoons chopped parsley, a handful of rocket
leaves and 2 tablespoons olive oil and mix together well.
Season to taste with salt and pepper and serve.

soy & orange salmon with noodles

Serves **4**

Preparation time **5 minutes**

Cooking time **10–15 minutes**

4 skinless **salmon fillets**, about 175 g (6 oz) each

spray **olive oil**, for oiling

250 g (8 oz) dried **soba noodles**

4 tablespoons **dark soy sauce**

2 tablespoons **orange juice**

2 tablespoons **mirin** (rice wine)

2 teaspoons **sesame oil**

2 tablespoons **sesame seeds**

Remove any bones from the salmon fillets and put the salmon in a bowl. Heat a heavy-based frying pan until hot and spray lightly with oil. Add the salmon and cook for 3–4 minutes on each side or until cooked through. Remove from the pan, wrap loosely in foil and leave to rest for 5 minutes.

Meanwhile, cook the noodles in a large saucepan of boiling water for about 5 minutes, or according to the packet instructions, until just tender.

While the noodles are cooking, mix together the soy sauce, orange juice and mirin in a bowl, then pour into the frying pan and bring to the boil. Reduce the heat and simmer for 1 minute.

Drain the noodles well, return to the pan and toss with the sesame oil and sprinkle over the seeds. Divide the salmon among 4 serving bowls and top with the sauce. Serve with steamed sugar snap peas.

For salmon, orange & soy parcels, put each salmon fillet on a 30 cm (12 inch) square of foil. Draw the foil edges up to form 'cups' and add the soy sauce, orange juice and mirin as above, along with 2 sliced spring onions, 2 sliced garlic cloves and 2 teaspoons peeled and grated fresh root ginger. Seal the edges of the foil together to form parcels, transfer to a baking sheet and bake in a preheated oven, 200°C (400°F), Gas Mark 6, for 15 minutes. Remove from the oven and leave to rest briefly, then serve with steamed rice.

mixed seafood grill

Serves **4**

Preparation time **10 minutes**, plus infusing

Cooking time **10 minutes**

300 g (10 oz) **ready-prepared squid**, cleaned

12 **raw prawns**, unpeeled

12 live **clams**, cleaned

12 live **mussels**, scrubbed and debearded

lemon wedges, to serve

Dressing

2 **garlic cloves**, peeled and bruised

6 tablespoons **extra virgin olive oil**

2 tablespoons chopped **parsley**

Cut down the side of the squid so that it can be laid flat on a chopping board. Using a sharp knife, lightly score the inside flesh in a crisscross pattern, then cut the squid into 3 cm (1 ¼ inch) squares. Chill until required.

Make the dressing. Put the garlic in a small bowl, add the oil and stir in the parsley. Leave the flavours to infuse for at least 15 minutes.

When ready to serve, heat a ridged griddle pan over a high heat until searing hot. Lightly brush the prawns and squid with half the dressing. Add the prawns to the pan and cook for 3–4 minutes on each side or until they turn pink. Transfer to a warmed serving platter.

Add the squid flesh (but not the tentacles), the clams and mussels to the pan (discarding any that don't shut when tapped), and cook for 5–7 minutes or until the squid turns white and is charred and the clams and mussels have opened. Discard any that remain closed. Add the squid tentacles and cook for 2–3 minutes more, then transfer everthing to the serving platter and drizzle all the seafood with the remaining dressing. Serve immediately with lemon wedges, avocado dip (see below) and bread, if liked.

For tangy avocado dip to serve as an accompaniment, halve, stone and peel 2 very ripe, large avocados and put in a food processor or blender with 2 tablespoons good-quality mayonnaise, 2 tablespoons soured cream, the juice of 1 lemon, 1 teaspoon mild chilli sauce, if liked, and some salt and pepper. Blend until smooth, spoon into a small bowl and place on the serving platter.

grilled sardines with tomato salsa

Serves **1**
Preparation time **10 minutes**
Cooking time **3–4 minutes**

3 **fresh sardines**, about
   125 g (4 oz) in total, gutted
4 tablespoons **lemon juice**
1 tablespoon chopped **basil**
salt and **pepper**

Tomato salsa
8 **cherry tomatoes**, chopped
1 **spring onion**, sliced
1 tablespoon chopped **basil**
½ **red pepper**, cored,
   deseeded and chopped

Make the tomato salsa by mixing together all the ingredients in a bowl.

Put the sardines on a baking sheet and drizzle with the lemon juice. Season to taste with salt and pepper. Cook the sardines under a preheated hot grill, turning once, for 3–4 minutes or until cooked through.

Sprinkle with the chopped basil and serve immediately with the tomato salsa and toasted ciabatta.

For quick sardine & anchovy toasts, cook the sardines as above, then put them in a food processor or blender with 50 g (2 oz) can anchovies in oil, drained, 1 crushed garlic clove, a sprig of parsley and 2 tablespoons olive oil. Whizz to a paste, then spread over slices of toasted ciabatta, sprinkle with chopped parsley and serve.

cod fillets with tomato & rocket

Serves **4**

Preparation time **5 minutes**

Cooking time **12–15 minutes**

4 chunky **cod fillets**, about
150 g (5 oz) each

3 tablespoons **olive oil**

2 **garlic cloves**, chopped

300 g (10 oz) **cherry
tomatoes on the vine**

2 tablespoons **balsamic
vinegar**

4 tablespoons chopped **basil**

125 g (4 oz) **rocket leaves**

salt and **pepper**

Rub the cod fillets all over with 1 tablespoon of the oil
and season well with salt and pepper. Scatter over the
garlic and put the fish in a roasting tin lined with baking
paper. Arrange the cherry tomatoes alongside and
drizzle with the remaining oil, the balsamic vinegar and
basil. Season with salt and pepper to taste.

Cook in a preheated oven, 220°C (425°F), Gas Mark 7,
for 12–15 minutes or until the fish is flaky and the
tomatoes are roasted. Serve the cod with the tomatoes
and rocket leaves.

For cod with Italian-style salsa, oil and season the
cod fillets as above and fry for 5–6 minutes or until
cooked through and golden brown. To make the salsa,
mix together 8 finely chopped sun-dried tomatoes,
2 tablespoons roughly chopped basil leaves,
1 tablespoon drained capers, 1 tablespoon lightly
crushed toasted pine nuts and 2 tablespoons olive
oil in a bowl. Serve with a rocket salad.

smoked trout & grape salad

Serves **2**
Preparation time **15 minutes**

200 g (7 oz) **smoked trout**
160 g (5½ oz) **red seedless grapes**
75 g (3 oz) **watercress**
1 **fennel bulb**

Dressing

3 tablespoons **mayonnaise**
4 **cornichons**, finely diced
1½ tablespoons **capers**, drained and chopped
2 tablespoons **lemon juice**
salt and **pepper**

Flake the smoked trout into bite-sized pieces, removing any bones and skin, and place in a large salad bowl. Wash and drain the grapes and watercress leaves and add them to the bowl. Finely slice the fennel and stir through the salad.

Make the dressing. Mix together the mayonnaise, cornichons, capers and lemon juice in a bowl. Season to taste with salt and pepper, then carefully mix through the salad and serve.

For crispy trout salad, prepare the dressing as above and add 1 finely chopped hard-boiled egg, 1 tablespoon chopped parsley and 2 finely chopped anchovy fillets. Prepare the salad as above (omitting the smoked trout) and adding 1 green apple, cut into matchsticks. Season 2 pieces of fresh trout, about 140 g (4½ oz) each, with salt and pepper. Heat 1 tablespoon vegetable oil in a frying pan over a high heat and cook the trout, skin side down, for 4 minutes, pressing it down with a fish slice to give an evenly crispy skin. Turn over the fish and cook for a further 2 minutes or until it is just cooked through. Toss the salad with the dressing and serve immediately with the crispy trout.

salmon fillets with sage & quinoa

Serves **4**
Preparation time **5 minutes**
Cooking time **15 minutes**

200 g (7 oz) **quinoa**
100 g (3½ oz) **butter**, at room
   temperature
8 **sage leaves**, chopped
small bunch of **chives**
grated rind and juice of
   1 **lemon**
4 **salmon fillets**, about
   175 g (6 oz) each
1 tablespoon **olive oil**
salt and **pepper**

Cook the quinoa in a saucepan of unsalted boiling water for about 15 minutes or according to the packet instructions until cooked but firm.

Meanwhile, mix together the butter, sage, chives and lemon rind in a small bowl and season to taste with salt and pepper.

Rub the salmon fillets with the oil, season with pepper and cook in a preheated frying pan, turning carefully once, for about 8–10 minutes or until cooked through and the salmon flakes easily. Remove from the pan and leave to rest.

Drain the quinoa, stir in the lemon juice and season to taste. Spoon on to serving plates and top with the salmon, topping each piece with a knob of sage butter.

For salmon with tarragon & couscous, replace the sage leaves with 4 sprigs of tarragon and the quinoa with 250 g (8 oz) couscous. Put the couscous in a heatproof bowl and pour over 400 ml (14 fl oz) boiling water. Cover and leave to stand for 5–8 minutes, or according to the packet instructions, until the liquid has been absorbed and the grains are soft. Fluff up with a fork and season. Dress with a little lemon juice and olive oil and serve with the salmon, as above.

vegetables

flatbread pizzas with blue cheese

Serves **4**
Preparation time **5 minutes**
Cooking time **7–8 minutes**

4 x 20 cm (8 inch)
  Mediterranean flatbreads
200 g (7 oz) **Gorgonzola**
  or **dolcelatte cheese**,
  crumbled
8 slices of **prosciutto**
50 g (2 oz) **rocket leaves**
extra virgin olive oil, for
  drizzling
pepper

Put the flatbreads on 2 baking sheets and scatter the centres with the blue cheese.

Bake in a preheated oven, 200°C (400°F), Gas Mark 6, for 7–8 minutes or until the bases are crisp and the cheese has melted.

Top the pizzas with the prosciutto and rocket leaves, season with pepper and drizzle with oil. Serve immediately.

For naan pizzas, put 4 naan breads on 2 baking sheets and spread 1 tablespoon passata (sieved tomatoes) over each one. Add 200 g (7 oz) sliced mozzarella cheese and top with some drained mixed mushroom antipasto from a jar and a few thyme leaves. Bake as above until the cheese has melted.

ricotta & red onion tortillas

Serves **1**
Preparation time **10 minutes**
Cooking time 4–**5 minutes**

40 g (1½ oz) **ricotta cheese**
½ **red onion**, thinly sliced
1 **tomato**, finely chopped
¼ **green chilli**, deseeded and
    finely chopped
1 tablespoon chopped **fresh**
    coriander
2 small **soft flour tortillas**
olive oil, for brushing

Mix together the ricotta, onion, tomato, chilli and coriander in a bowl.

Heat a ridged griddle pan until hot. Brush the tortillas with a little oil, add to the pan and cook very briefly on each side.

Spread half the ricotta mixture over one half of each tortilla and fold over the other half to cover. Serve immediately with a green salad.

For Mexican quesadillas, mix together ½ cored, deseeded and chopped red pepper, 1 finely sliced spring onion, 25 g (1 oz) grated Cheddar cheese, 3 pieces of drained jalapeño pepper from a jar and 1 tablespoon chopped fresh coriander in a bowl. Spread the mixture on 1 tortilla and place the other tortilla on top. Place in a nonstick frying pan and cook over a medium heat until the cheese melts. Flip over and cook on the other side for a few more minutes. Slide on to a plate, cut into quarters and serve with guacamole and soured cream.

broad bean & goats' cheese salad

Serves **4**

Preparation time **10 minutes**

Cooking time **15–20 minutes**

250 g (8 oz) **ripe tomatoes**

2 **garlic cloves**, peeled

5 tablespoons **extra virgin olive oil**

1 tablespoon good-quality **aged balsamic vinegar**

300 g (10 oz) fresh or frozen **broad beans**

300 g (10 oz) **dried farfalle**

200 g (7 oz) **goats' cheese**, crumbled

20 **basil leaves**, torn

salt and **pepper**

Put the tomatoes and garlic in a food processor or blender and whizz until the tomatoes are finely chopped. Tip into a large bowl and stir in the oil and vinegar. Season with salt and pepper.

Cook the broad beans in a saucepan of boiling water until tender (6–8 minutes for fresh broad beans or 2 minutes for frozen). Drain, refresh under cold running water and drain again. Peel off the skins. Stir the beans into the tomato mixture and leave them to marinate while you cook the pasta.

Cook the pasta in a large saucepan of salted boiling water according to the packet instructions until al dente. Drain, refresh under cold running water and drain again.

Stir the pasta into the tomato and broad bean mixture. Add the goats' cheese and basil, then toss gently. Season to taste with salt and pepper. Leave to stand for at least 5 minutes before serving.

For fresh soya bean & pecorino farfalle salad,

prepare the tomato and garlic mixture as above, replacing the broad beans with 250 g (8 oz) frozen or fresh soya beans, cooked for 3 minutes. Cook the pasta as above and stir into the soya bean mixture. Omit the goats' cheese and basil and stir in 60 g (2¼ oz) shaved pecorino cheese and 3 tablespoons finely chopped mint or parsley.

vegetable & tofu stir-fry

Serves **4**
Preparation time **10 minutes**
Cooking time **7 minutes**

3 tablespoons **sunflower oil**
300 g (10 oz) **firm tofu**, cubed
1 **onion**, sliced
2 **carrots**, sliced
150 g (5 oz) **broccoli**, broken
  into small florets and stalks
  sliced
1 **red pepper**, cored,
  deseeded and sliced
1 large **courgette**, sliced
150 g (5 oz) **sugar snap peas**
2 tablespoons **soy sauce**
2 tablespoons **sweet chilli
  sauce**
125 ml (4 fl oz) **water**

To garnish
chopped **red chillies**
Thai or ordinary **basil leaves**

Heat 1 tablespoon of the oil in a wok or large frying pan until starting to smoke, add the tofu and stir-fry over a high heat for 2 minutes or until golden. Remove with a slotted spoon and keep warm.

Heat the remaining oil in the pan, add the onion and carrots and stir-fry for 1½ minutes. Add the broccoli and red pepper and stir-fry for 1 minute, then add the courgette and sugar snap peas and stir-fry for 1 minute.

Mix together the soy and chilli sauces and measurement water and add to the pan with the tofu. Cook for 1 minute. Serve in bowls, garnished with chopped red chillies and basil leaves.

For vegetable & cashew stir-fry, heat 1 tablespoon sunflower oil in a wok or large frying pan, add 2 red chillies, deseeded and sliced, 2 onions, cut into thin wedges and ¼ teaspoon freshly ground black pepper and cook for 2 minutes. Add the vegetables as above and stir-fry until tender. Toss through 2 tablespoons soy sauce and 1 tablespoon sugar. Sprinkle with basil leaves and 200 g (7 oz) toasted cashew nuts. Serve immediately with jasmine rice.

sweetcorn & pepper frittata

Serves **4**

Preparation time **10 minutes**

Cooking time about **10 minutes**

2 tablespoons **olive oil**

4 **spring onions**, thinly sliced

200 g (7 oz) can **sweetcorn**, drained

150 g (5 oz) bottled **roasted red peppers** in oil, drained and cut into strips

4 **eggs**, lightly beaten

125 g (4 oz) strong **Cheddar cheese**, grated

small handful of **chives**, finely chopped

salt and **pepper**

Heat the oil in a frying pan with an ovenproof handle, add the spring onions, sweetcorn and red peppers, and cook for 30 seconds.

Add the eggs, Cheddar, chives and salt and pepper to taste and cook over a medium heat for 4–5 minutes or until the base is set.

Place the pan under a preheated hot grill and cook the omelette for 3–4 minutes or until golden and set. Cut into wedges and serve immediately with a green salad and crusty bread.

For courgette, pepper & Gruyère frittata, cook the spring onion and red peppers as above, replacing the sweetcorn with 200 g (7 oz) finely chopped courgettes. Add the eggs, 125 g (4 oz) grated Gruyère cheese (instead of the Cheddar) 4 tablespoons chopped mint (instead of the chives), season and cook as above.

green curry with straw mushrooms

Serves **4**
Preparation time **10 minutes**
Cooking time **10 minutes**

300 ml (½ pint) **coconut milk**,
  plus extra for drizzling
40 g (1½ oz) **green curry
  paste**
300 ml (½ pint) **vegetable
  stock**
2 **aubergines**, roughly
  chopped into large chunks
40 g (1½ oz) **soft brown
  sugar**
4 teaspoons **soy sauce**
25 g (1 oz) **fresh root ginger**,
  peeled and finely chopped
425 g (14 oz) can **straw
  mushrooms**, drained
50 g (2 oz) **green pepper**,
  cored, deseeded and thinly
  sliced
salt

Put the coconut milk and curry paste in a saucepan over a medium heat and stir well. Pour in the stock, then add the aubergines, sugar, soy sauce, ginger, and salt to taste.

Bring to the boil and cook, stirring, for 5 minutes. Add the mushrooms and green pepper, reduce the heat and cook for 2 minutes until piping hot.

Serve in bowls, drizzled with a little extra coconut milk.

For vegetable korma, heat 1 tablespoon vegetable oil in a large saucepan, add 1 finely diced onion, 3 bruised cardamom pods, 2 teaspoons each of ground cumin and ground coriander and ½ teaspoon turmeric and cook over a low heat for 5–6 minutes or until the onion is light golden. Add 1 deseeded and chopped green chilli, 1 crushed garlic clove and a thumb-sized piece of fresh root ginger, peeled and grated, and cook for 1 minute, then add a selection of 425 g (14 oz) prepared mixed vegetables, such as cauliflower, peppers, carrots and courgettes, and cook for a further 5 minutes. Remove the pan from the heat and stir through 200 ml (7 fl oz) yogurt and 2 tablespoons ground almonds. Serve sprinkled with chopped coriander and accompanied with basmati rice.

panzanella salad

Serves **4**

Preparation time **15 minutes**, plus standing

600 g (1¼ lb) large **tomatoes**
1 tablespoon **sea salt**
150 g (5 oz) **ciabatta bread**
½ **red onion**, finely chopped
handful of **basil leaves**, plus extra to garnish
1 tablespoon **red wine vinegar**
2 tablespoons **olive oil**
12 pickled **white anchovies**, drained
salt and **pepper**

Roughly chop the tomatoes into 1.5 cm (¾ inch) pieces and put them in a non-metallic bowl. Sprinkle over the sea salt and leave to stand for 1 hour.

Remove the crusts from the ciabatta and tear the bread into rough chunks.

Give the tomatoes a good squash with clean hands, then add the bread, onion, basil, vinegar and oil. Season to taste with salt and pepper. Mix together carefully and transfer to serving plates. Garnish with the drained anchovies and basil leaves and serve.

For tomato & bean salad, finely slice 1 red onion, cover with 4 tablespoons red wine vinegar and leave to stand for about 30 minutes. Cut 150 g (5 oz) ciabatta bread into chunks and place in a roasting tin. Drizzle with olive oil, season with salt and pepper and add 2 sprigs of thyme. Cook the ciabatta in a preheated oven, 190°C (375°F), Gas Mark 5, for 8 minutes or until golden and crispy. Dice 300 g (10 oz) tomatoes and put them in a large bowl. Add a drained 400 g (13 oz) can borlotti beans, a drained 400 g (13 oz) can cannellini beans and 1 bunch of chopped basil. Remove the onion from the vinegar, reserving the vinegar, and add to the salad with 12 drained pickled white anchovies. Add 1 teaspoon Dijon mustard to the reserved vinegar and whisk in 5 tablespoons olive oil. Season with salt and pepper. Add the dressing to the salad, toss thoroughly and serve garnished with the ciabatta croûtons.

curried couscous salad

Serves **4**
Preparation time **15 minutes**

juice of **1 orange**
2 teaspoons **mild curry paste**
200 g (7 oz) **couscous**
50 g (2 oz) **sultanas**
300 ml (½ pint) **boiling water**
250 g (8 oz) **smoked mackerel fillets**
1 small **red onion**, finely chopped
½ **red pepper**, cored, deseeded and diced
2 **tomatoes**, chopped
small bunch of **fresh coriander**, roughly chopped
pepper

Put the orange juice and curry paste into a heatproof bowl and stir together. Add the couscous, sultanas and a little pepper, then pour over the boiling water and fork together. Cover and leave to stand for 5 minutes or according to the packet instructions until the liquid has been absorbed.

Meanwhile, peel the skin off the mackerel fillets and break the flesh into large flakes, discarding any bones.

Add the mackerel, onion, red pepper and tomatoes to the couscous and fork together lightly. Sprinkle the chopped coriander over the top, spoon on to plates and serve immediately.

For curried couscous salad with lamb cutlets, mix together 4 tablespoons natural yogurt and 1 teaspoon mild curry paste in a non-metallic dish. Add 12 lamb cutlets and coat evenly in the mixture. Prepare the couscous salad as above, omitting the mackerel. Heat 2 tablespoons vegetable oil in a large griddle pan over a high heat, add the lamb and fry for 3 minutes on each side or until cooked through. Serve the lamb on the couscous salad, garnished with chopped coriander.

red pepper & cheese tortellini

Serves **4**

Preparation time **10 minutes**, plus cooling

Cooking time **15 minutes**

2 **red peppers**
2 **garlic cloves**, chopped
8 **spring onions**, finely sliced
500 g (1 lb) **fresh cheese-stuffed tortellini** or any other fresh stuffed tortellini
175 ml (6 fl oz) **olive oil**
25 g (1 oz) **Parmesan cheese**, finely grated
salt and **pepper**

Cut the peppers into large pieces, removing the cores and seeds. Lay skin side up on a grill pan and cook under a preheated grill until the skin blackens and blisters. Transfer to a plastic bag, tie the top to enclose and leave to cool, then peel away the skin.

Place the peppers and garlic in a food processor or blender and blend until fairly smooth. Stir in the spring onions and set aside.

Cook the tortellini in a large saucepan of boiling water according to the packet instructions until al dente. Drain and return to the pan.

Stir the pepper mixture into the pasta, add the oil and Parmesan and toss together. Season to taste with salt and pepper and serve immediately.

For warm ham & red pepper tortellini salad, grill and peel the red peppers as above, then thinly slice the flesh. While the tortellini is cooking, thinly slice 1 red onion. Drain the pasta and toss with 125 g (4 oz) chopped cooked ham, 200 g (7 oz) rocket leaves and the onion and red peppers. Serve immediately.

mushroom stroganoff

Serves **4**

Preparation time **10 minutes**

Cooking time **10 minutes**

15 g (½ oz) **butter**

2 tablespoons **olive oil**

1 **onion,** thinly sliced

4 **garlic cloves,** finely chopped

500 g (1 lb) **chestnut mushrooms,** sliced

2 tablespoons **wholegrain mustard**

250 ml (8 fl oz) **crème fraîche**

salt and **pepper**

3 tablespoons chopped **parsley,** to garnish

Heat the butter and oil in a large frying pan, add the onion and garlic and fry gently until softened and beginning to brown.

Add the mushrooms to the pan and cook until softened and beginning to brown. Stir in the mustard and crème fraîche and just heat through. Season to taste with salt and pepper, then serve immediately, garnished with the chopped parsley.

For mushroom soup with garlic croûtons, cook

the mushrooms as above. Remove the crusts from 2 thick slices of day-old white bread and rub with 2 halved garlic cloves. Cut the bread into cubes. Fry the cubes of bread in a shallow depth of vegetable oil in a frying pan, turning continuously, for 5 minutes or until browned all over and crisp. Drain on kitchen paper. After adding the mustard and crème fraîche to the mushroom mixture as above, add 400 ml (14 fl oz) boiling vegetable stock, then purée the mixture in a food processor or blender until smooth. Serve in warmed bowls, topped with the croûtons and garnished with the chopped parsley.

cheesy polenta & mushrooms

Serves **4**
Preparation time **10 minutes**
Cooking time **15 minutes**

400 g (13 oz) **mixed
wild mushrooms,** such
as porcini, girolles and
chanterelles
25 g (1 oz) **butter**
2 **garlic cloves,** chopped
5 whole **sage leaves**
50 ml (2 fl oz) **dry vermouth**
salt and **pepper**

Polenta
750 ml (1 ¼ pints) **water**
200 g (7 oz) **instant polenta**
50 g (2 oz) **Parmesan
cheese,** freshly grated
50 g (2 oz) **butter,** cubed

Brush away any soil and grit from the mushrooms with
a moist cloth, then slice the porcini and tear any other
large mushrooms in half. Set aside.

Melt the butter in a large frying pan over a medium-
high heat. Add the garlic, sage and the dense, tougher
mushrooms and cook for 2–3 minutes. Add the
remaining mushrooms, season with salt and pepper and
cook for 2–3 minutes until soft and cooked through.
Pour in the vermouth and cook, stirring, for 1 minute.

For the polenta, bring the measurement water to the
boil in a large, heavy-based saucepan. Put the polenta
in a jug and pour into the water in a slow but steady
stream, stirring vigorously with a wooden spoon to
prevent any lumps forming. Reduce the heat to a
slow simmer and cook, stirring frequently, for about
5 minutes, or until the polenta is thick and comes away
from the side of the pan. Stir in the butter and season
with salt and pepper.

Divide the polenta between 4 serving plates, then top
with the mushrooms.

For cheesy polenta with mushrooms & tomato,
cook the mushrooms as above, but replace the
rosemary with 3 chopped thyme sprigs and use 150 ml
(¼ pint) full-bodied red wine instead of the vermouth.
When the wine has boiled for 1 minute, stir in 300 ml
(½ pint) passata. Season with salt and pepper and bring
to the boil, then simmer for 5 minutes. Cook the polenta
as above, then gradually stir in the cheese. Serve with
the mushroom and tomato mixture.

spring garden pasta salad

Serves **4**
Preparation time **10 minutes**,
   plus cooling
Cooking time **10 minutes**

4 tablespoons **extra virgin
   olive oil**
1 **garlic clove**, crushed
finely grated rind and juice of
   ½ **lemon**
6 **spring onions**, thinly sliced
175 g (6 oz) **dried fusilli**
150 g (5 oz) **asparagus tips**,
   cut into 2.5 cm (1 inch)
   pieces
150 g (5 oz) **green beans**,
   trimmed and cut into 2.5 cm
   (1 inch) pieces
50g (2 oz) fresh or frozen
   peas
1 **buffalo mozzarella cheese
   ball**, drained and torn into
   small pieces
50 g (2 oz) **watercress**
2 tablespoons roughly
   chopped **parsley**
2 tablespoons snipped **chives**
8 **basil leaves**, torn
salt and **pepper**

Mix the oil, garlic, lemon rind and juice and spring onions together in a large, non-metallic serving bowl and leave to infuse while you cook the pasta.

Cook the pasta in a large saucepan of salted boiling water according to the packet instructions until al dente, adding the asparagus, beans and peas 3 minutes before the end of the cooking time.

Drain the pasta and vegetables lightly, then stir into the prepared dressing. Set aside in a cool place until cooled to room temperature.

Stir the remaining ingredients into the pasta salad. Season with salt and pepper, then leave the dish to stand for at least 5 minutes for the flavours to mingle before serving.

For sugar snap pea & broad bean salad, make the dressing and cook the pasta as above, replacing the asparagus tips with 150 g (5 oz) sugar snap peas and the green beans with 150 g (5 oz) broad beans. Cut the sugar snap peas in half and add them, together with the beans, to the pan 3–5 minutes before the end of the pasta cooking time. Replace the watercress with 50 g (2 oz) rocket.

mango curry

Serves **4**

Preparation time **10 minutes**

Cooking time **8–10 minutes**

1 tablespoon **vegetable oil**

1 teaspoon **mustard seeds**

1 **onion**, halved and thinly
sliced

15–20 **curry leaves**, fresh or
dried

½ teaspoon **dried red chilli
flakes**

1 teaspoon peeled and grated
fresh root ginger

1 **green chilli**, deseeded and
sliced

1 teaspoon **ground turmeric**

3 ripe **mangoes**, peeled,
stoned and thinly sliced

400 ml (14 fl oz) **natural
yogurt**, lightly beaten

salt

Heat the oil in a large saucepan until hot, add the
mustard seeds, onion, curry leaves and chilli flakes
and fry, stirring, for 4–5 minutes or until the onion is
lightly browned.

Add the ginger and chilli and stir-fry for 1 minute,
then add the turmeric and stir to mix well.

Remove the pan from the heat, add the mangoes
and yogurt and stir continuously until well mixed.
Season to taste with salt.

Return the pan to a low heat and heat through for
1 minute, stirring continuously. (Do not let it boil or
the curry will curdle.) Serve immediately with
4 warm chapattis.

For aubergine & pea curry, heat 3 tablespoons
sunflower oil in a large frying pan until hot, then
add 4 peeled and cubed medium-sized potatoes,
1 aubergine, cut into small chunks, 150 g (5 oz)
frozen peas, 2 finely sliced onions, 2 crushed garlic
cloves, 1 tablespoon ginger paste and 2 tablespoons
medium curry powder. Stir-fry for 3–4 minutes or
until the onion has softened and is turning golden,
then pour in 600 ml (1 pint) chicken or vegetable
stock and cook for 10–15 minutes or until the stock
has reduced. Stir in 150 ml (¼ pint) crème fraîche
and serve with naan bread.

asparagus & taleggio pizza

Serves **2**
Preparation time **5 minutes**
Cooking time **10 minutes**

5 tablespoons **passata** (sieved
    tomatoes)
1 tablespoon **red pesto**
pinch of **salt**
1 large ready-made **garlic
    pizza bread**
250 g (8 oz) **Taleggio cheese**,
    derinded and sliced
250 g (8 oz) **cherry tomatoes**,
    halved
175 g (6 oz) **fine asparagus
    spears**, trimmed
2 tablespoons **olive oil**
pepper
a few **basil** leaves

Mix together the passata, pesto and salt in a small bowl and spread the mixture over the top of the garlic pizza bread. Top with the Taleggio, cherry tomatoes and asparagus spears and drizzle with the oil.

Bake the pizza directly on the oven shelf or on a pizza tray at the top of a preheated oven, 200°C (400°F), Gas Mark 6, for 10 minutes or until the asparagus is tender and the pizza base is crisp. Grind some pepper over the top and scatter over basil leaves before serving.

For artichoke, egg & Parma ham pizza, omit the red pesto and spread the passata and salt over the pizza bread as above, then top with a 400 g (13 oz) can artichoke hearts, drained and quartered, 8 slices of Parma ham torn into shreds and 3 handfuls of chopped pitted black olives. Break a small egg into the centre of the pizza, then top with 250 g (8 oz) torn mozzarella pieces and some basil leaves. Bake as above.

sweet treats

heavenly chocolate puddings

Serves **4**
Preparation time **10 minutes**
Cooking time **10 minutes**

100 g (3½ oz) **milk chocolate**, broken up
50 g (2 oz) **unsalted butter**
40 g (1½ oz) **cocoa powder**
75 g (3 oz) **golden caster sugar**
2 **eggs**, separated
1 teaspoon **vanilla extract**
4 tablespoons **single cream**
icing sugar, for dusting

Melt the chocolate and butter in a large mixing bowl placed over a pan of barely simmering water, making sure the surface of the water does not touch the bowl. Remove from the heat, add the cocoa powder, 50 g (2 oz) of the sugar, the egg yolks, vanilla extract and cream and beat the mixture to a smooth paste.

Whisk the egg whites in a clean bowl until peaking and gradually whisk in the remaining sugar. Use a large metal spoon to fold a quarter of the meringue into the chocolate mixture to lighten it, then fold in the remainder.

Spoon the mixture into 4 small ramekin dishes or similar-sized ovenproof dishes. Bake in a preheated oven, 160°C (325°F), Gas Mark 3, for 8–10 minutes or until a very thin crust has formed over the surface. Dust with icing sugar and serve immediately.

For boozy chocolate puddings, stir 2 tablespoons brandy, rum or orange liqueur into the mixture with the cream. Continue as above.

cherry & cinnamon zabaglione

Serves **4**
Preparation time **10 minutes**
Cooking time about
 12 minutes

4 **egg yolks**
125 g (4 oz) **caster sugar**
150 ml (¼ pint) **cream sherry**
large pinch of **ground
 cinnamon**, plus extra to
 decorate
400 g (13 oz) can **black
 cherries in syrup**

Pour 5 cm (2 inches) water into a medium saucepan and bring to the boil. Set a large heatproof bowl over the pan, making sure that the water does not touch the base of the bowl. Reduce the heat so that the water is simmering, then add the egg yolks, sugar, sherry and cinnamon to the bowl. Whisk for 5–8 minutes or until very thick and foamy and the custard leaves a trail when the whisk is lifted above the mixture.

Drain off some of the cherry syrup and then tip the cherries and just a little of the syrup into a small saucepan. Warm through, then spoon into 4 glasses. Pour the warm zabaglione over the top and serve dusted with cinnamon and with amaretti biscuits.

For raspberry zabaglione, put 225 g (7 ½ oz) raspberries, reserving 12 for decoration, in a food processor or blender with a squeeze of lemon juice and blitz to a purée. Push through a sieve to remove the seeds and set aside. Make the zabaglione as above and when ready pour into 4 glasses. Swirl through the raspberry purée to create a ripple effect and decorate with the reserved raspberries. Serve with biscotti.

spiced bananas

Serves **8**
Preparation time **10 minutes**
Cooking time **10 minutes**

8 **bananas**, peeled
2 tablespoons **lemon juice**
8 tablespoons **light muscavado sugar**
50 g (2 oz) **butter**, softened
1 teaspoon **cinnamon**

Rum mascarpone cream
250 g (8 oz) **mascarpone cheese**
2 tablespoons **rum**
1–2 tablespoons **granulated sugar**

Put each banana on a double piece of foil. Drizzle over the lemon juice and sprinkle 1 tablespoon of the brown sugar on each banana.

Beat together the butter and cinnamon in a bowl until creamy, then spoon over the bananas. Wrap each banana tightly in the foil and cook over a barbecue or under a preheated medium grill for 10 minutes.

Meanwhile, make the rum mascarpone cream. Mix together the mascarpone, rum and sugar in a bowl.

Unwrap the bananas and slice thickly. Serve immediately with the rum mascarpone cream.

For BBQ pineapple with rum butter glaze, cut off the top and base of 1 large fresh pineapple and slice off the skin, then cut into quarters and remove the core from each quarter. Slice the quarters across into 2.5 cm (1 inch) thick triangular slices. Sprinkle both sides with a little caster sugar and cook over a barbecue for 5–6 minutes or until lightly caramelized. Meanwhile, melt 75g (3 oz) butter in a small pan, then add 75g (3 oz) demerara sugar and the juice of ½ lime. Scrape out the seeds of 1 vanilla pod and add to the pan with 2 tablespoons dark rum. Stir until the mixture has melted and bubbled to form a smooth glaze. Place the pineapple slices on a plate, spoon over the rum butter and serve immediately with ice cream.

italian trifle

Serves **4**

Preparation **10 minutes**, plus
 cooling and chilling

Cooking time **10 minutes**

8 **sponge fingers**

2 tablespoons **blueberry jam**

50 ml (2 fl oz) **sweet sherry** or
 sweet white wine

250 g (8 oz) **blueberries**

300 ml (½ pint) **milk**

1 tablespoon **cornflour**

2 **egg yolks**

2 tablespoons **caster sugar**

300 ml (½ pint) **whipping
 cream**

50 g (2 oz) **plain dark
 chocolate**, grated

Spread the sponge fingers with the blueberry jam and put in a glass bowl. Sprinkle over the sherry or white wine and half of the blueberries.

Mix a little of the milk with the cornflour until smooth. Stir into the rest of the milk. Pour into a saucepan and bring to the boil, stirring continuously as the milk thickens. When it is boiling and smooth, remove the pan from the heat.

Whisk the egg yolks and sugar in a bowl until light and creamy. Add the milk slowly, whisking all the time. Mix well, pour over the blueberries and sponge fingers, then sprinkle the rest of the blueberries over the top. Leave to cool, then chill, preferably overnight.

When ready to serve, whip the cream until softly peaking and spread it over the trifle. Sprinkle the grated chocolate over the top.

For fresh citrus trifle, mix together the juice of 3 oranges and 75 ml (3 fl oz) limoncello in a bowl. Put the sponge fingers in a glass bowl and pour over the orange mixture. Make the custard mixture as above, pour over the sponge and leave to cool. Chill as above. When ready to serve, spread with the whipped cream and decorate with 1 punnet raspberries and shavings of plain dark chocolate.

pancake stack with maple syrup

Serves **4**
Preparation time **10 minutes**
Cooking time **6 minutes**

1 **egg**
100 g (3½ oz) **strong plain flour**
125 ml (4 fl oz) **milk**
2½ tablespoons **vegetable oil**
1 tablespoon **caster sugar**
maple syrup, for drizzling

Put the egg, flour, milk, oil and sugar in a food processor or blender and blend until the mixture is smooth and creamy.

Heat a large frying pan over a medium heat and put in 4 half-ladlefuls of the batter to make 4 pancakes. After about 1 minute the tops of the pancakes will start to set and air bubbles will rise to the top and burst. Use a spatula to turn the pancakes over and cook on the other side for 1 minute. Repeat twice more until you have used all the batter and made 12 small pancakes in total.

Bring the pancakes to the table as a stack, drizzled with maple syrup, and serve 3 pancakes to each person, with scoops of ice cream.

For orange-flavoured pancakes, make a batter as above but with 125 g (4 oz) plain flour, 2 teaspoons each caster sugar and grated orange rind, 1 teaspoon each cream of tartar and golden syrup, ½ teaspoon each salt and bicarbonate of soda, 1 egg, 125 ml (4 fl oz) warm milk and a few drops of orange essence. Cook the pancakes as above.

passion fruit yogurt fool

6 passion fruit
300 ml (½ pint) **Greek yogurt**
1 tablespoon **clear honey**
200 ml (7 fl oz) **whipping cream**
4 pieces of **shortbread**, to serve

Halve the passion fruit and remove the flesh and seeds. Put the yogurt in a bowl, then stir in the flesh and seeds with the honey.

Whip the cream until softly peaking, then fold into the yogurt mixture.

Spoon into tall glasses and serve with the shortbread.

For mango & lime yogurt fool, omit the passion fruit, instead puréeing 1 large ripe peeled and stoned mango with the grated rind of 1 lime and icing sugar to taste. Mix into the yogurt, omitting the honey, and fold in the whipped cream.

warm, nutty chocolate fondue

Serves **4**
Preparation time **15 minutes**
Cooking time **10 minutes**

100 g (3½ oz) **bar Toblerone
   chocolate**
50 g (2 oz) **plain dark
   chocolate**
1 tablespoon **rum**
2 tablespoons **double cream**

To serve
selection of **fruit**, such as
   strawberries, cherries and
   sliced banana
cookies

Melt the Toblerone and dark chocolate in a heatproof
bowl set over a saucepan of gently simmering water.
When melted, add the rum and cream, and continue to
heat, stirring, for 1 minute.

Pour the chocolate mixture into a fondue pot and keep
warm on a burner. Dip a selection of fruits and cookies
into the chocolate and enjoy.

For butterscotch fondue, melt 100 g (3½ oz) soft
light brown sugar, 4 tablespoons vanilla caster sugar,
300 g (10 oz) golden syrup and 65 g (2½ oz) unsalted
butter in a saucepan, then boil for 5 minutes. Add
250 ml (8 fl oz) double cream and ½ teaspoon vanilla
extract and stir together, then remove the pan from
the heat. Pour into a fondue pot and serve with fruit
as above.

pears with minted mascarpone

Serves **4**

Preparation time **10 minutes**

Cooking time **5 minutes**

30 g (1¼ oz) **unsalted butter**

2 tablespoons **clear honey**

4 ripe **dessert pears**, such
as Red William, cored and
quartered lengthways

lemon juice, for sprinkling

Minted mascarpone

1 tablespoon finely chopped
mint

1 tablespoon **granulated
sugar**

175 g (6 oz) **mascarpone
cheese**

To decorate

mint sprigs

sifted **icing sugar**

ground cinnamon

Melt the butter in a small saucepan. Remove the pan
from the heat and stir in the honey.

Sprinkle the pear slices with a little lemon juice as
soon as they are cut to prevent them from discolouring.
Line a baking sheet with foil and lay the pear slices on
it. Brush the pears with the butter and honey mixture
and cook under a preheated grill on its highest setting
for 5 minutes.

Meanwhile, make the minted mascarpone. Lightly
whisk the mint and granulated sugar into the
mascarpone in a bowl.

Arrange the pear slices on 4 plates and top each with a
spoonful of the minted mascarpone. Decorate with mint
sprigs, then lightly dust with icing sugar and cinnamon
and serve immediately.

For pear & jam tarts, lay out a 300 g (10 oz) packet of
ready-rolled puff pastry, thawed if frozen, on a floured
surface and cut out 4 circles using an 18 cm (7 inch)
plate as a template. Transfer the circles to 2 greased
baking sheets. Peel, core and finely slice the pears and
place in a bowl. Toss with just enough caster sugar
to coat the fruit and 2 tablespoons freshly squeezed
orange juice. Place 1 tablespoon any flavoured jam
jam in the middle of each pastry circle, fan out the fruit
slices on top and fold in the sides of the pastry to hold it
all together. Bake in a preheated oven, 220°C (425°F),
Gas Mark 7, for 10–12 minutes until the fruit has
softened and the pastry is crisp and golden. Serve with
vanilla ice cream.

pain perdu with mixed berries

Serves **4**
Preparation time **10 minutes**
Cooking time **10 minutes**

4 thick slices of **brioche**
2 **eggs**
6 tablespoons **milk**
50 g (2 oz) **unsalted butter**
150 g (5 oz) **Greek yogurt**
250 g (8 oz) **raspberries**
100 g (3½ oz) **blueberries**
icing sugar, for dusting, or
  maple syrup, for drizzling

Cut each slice of brioche into 2 triangles. Beat the eggs and milk in a shallow bowl with a fork.

Heat half the butter in a largefrying pan. Quickly dip the bread, a triangle at a time, into the egg mixture, then put as many as you can get into the frying pan. Cook over a medium heat until the underside is golden. Turn over and cook the second side, then remove from the pan and keep warm. Heat the remaining butter in the pan and dip and cook the remaining brioche triangles.

Transfer the cooked triangles to 4 serving plates, top with spoonfuls of yogurt, a scattering of berries and a light dusting of sifted icing sugar or a drizzle of maple syrup. Serve immediately.

For spiced pain perdu with apricots, simmer 150 g (5 oz) ready-to-eat dried apricots with the juice of 1 orange and 125 ml (4 fl oz) water for 10 minutes or until tender. Cut 4 slices of fruit bread in half. Beat the egg and milk as above with ¼ teaspoon ground cinnamon, then dip and fry the fruit bread as above. Arrange on plates with spoonfuls of Greek yogurt and the warm apricot compôte.

sweet chestnut mess

Serves **4**
Preparation time **15 minutes**

250 g (8 oz) **fromage frais**
1 tablespoon **icing sugar**,
   sifted
100 g (3½ oz) **sweetened
   chestnut purée**
100 g (3½ oz) **meringues**,
   crushed
plain dark chocolate shards,
   to decorate

Beat together the fromage frais and icing sugar in a large bowl. Stir in half the chestnut purée and the crushed meringues.

Spoon the remaining chestnut purée into 4 individual serving dishes and top with the meringue mess. Decorate with the chocolate shards and serve.

For sweet chestnut pancakes, stir all the chestnut purée into the fromage frais. Heat 8 ready-made pancakes according to the packet instructions and spread them with the chestnut purée mixture. Roll them up and dust with cocoa powder and icing sugar.

caramelized blueberry custards

Serves **6**

Preparation time **10 minutes**,
  plus cooling

Cooking time **5 minutes**

150 g (5 oz) **granulated
  sugar**

3 tablespoons **cold water**

2 tablespoons **boiling water**

150 g (5 oz) fresh (not frozen)
  blueberries

400 g (13 oz) **fromage frais**

425 g (14 oz) can or carton
  custard

Put the sugar and measurement cold water into a frying pan and heat gently, stirring very occasionally, until the sugar has completely dissolved. Bring to the boil, then cook for 3–4 minutes, without stirring, until the syrup is just changing colour and is golden around the edges.

Add the measurement boiling water, standing well back as the syrup will spit, then tilt the pan to mix. Add the blueberries and cook for 1 minute. Remove the pan from the heat and leave to cool slightly.

Mix the fromage frais and custard together, spoon into 6 small dishes, then spoon the blueberry mixture over the top. Serve immediately with baby meringues, if liked.

For banana custards, make the caramel as above, then add 2 sliced bananas instead of the blueberries. Cool slightly, then spoon over the custard and fromage frais mixture. Decorate with grated plain dark chocolate.

tiramisu with raspberry surprise

Serves **4**
Preparation time **15 minutes**,
  plus chilling

6 tablespoons very strong
  espresso coffee
3 tablespoons **grappa** or
  brandy
16 **sponge fingers**
175 g (6 oz) **mascarpone
  cheese**
2 **eggs**, separated
50 g (2 oz) **icing sugar**
200 g (8 oz) **raspberries**
25 g (1 oz) **plain dark
  chocolate**

Stir together the coffee and grappa or brandy in a bowl.
Dip the sponge fingers into the liquid to coat evenly,
then arrange half of them in the base of a small shallow
dish or serving platter, pouring over any excess liquid.

Whisk together the mascarpone, egg yolks and icing
sugar in a bowl until smooth and well blended. In a
separate clean bowl, whisk the egg whites until stiff and
glossy, then fold the egg whites and the mascarpone
mixture together until well blended.

Spoon half the mixture over the soaked sponge fingers
and smooth the surface. Scatter half the raspberries
over the top. Repeat with another layer of sponge
fingers, followed by the rest of the marscarpone mixture
and finish with the remaining raspberries on top. Grate
the chocolate straight on to the mixture. Cover and chill,
preferably overnight, until set.

For winter gold tiramisu, replace the grappa or brandy
with 2 tablespoons Grand Marnier, and the raspberries
with the juice of 1 large orange. When whisking the
mascarpone with the egg yolks and icing sugar, add the
grated rind of 1 orange. Continue as above, replacing
the plain dark chocolate with a dark, spicy, orange-
flavoured chocolate.

almond brittle

Serves **8**
Preparation time **5 minutes**,
  plus cooling
Cooking time **10 minutes**

250 g (8 oz) **blanched
  almonds**
250 g (8 oz) **sugar**
4 tablespoons **water**

Line a baking sheet with nonstick baking paper.

Put the almonds on a grill pan and toast under a preheated grill until lightly brown. Leave to cool slightly, then roughly chop.

Heat a nonstick frying pan over a low heat, add the sugar and measurement water, and dissolve, without stirring, until it has melted and turned golden brown. Take care that the heat is not too high or the caramel will burn and have a very bitter taste.

Stir in the almonds, then pour the mixture on to the prepared baking sheet. Leave to cool, then break into small pieces and store in an airtight container until required. Serve with ice cream or good strong coffee.

For French almond mendiants, melt 200 g (7 oz) plain dark chocolate in a heatproof bowl set over a saucepan of gently simmering water. Spoon teaspoonfuls of the melted mixture on to a baking sheet lined with nonstick baking paper. Using the back of a spoon, shape into small discs, then sprinkle each disc with a few blanched almonds and some dried fruits. Leave to set in a cool place (ideally, not a refrigerator) before serving.

spiced infused fruit salad

Serves **6**
Preparation time **15 minutes**
Cooking time **5 minutes**

1 **vanilla pod**
175 ml (6 fl oz) **water**
2½ tablespoons **caster sugar**
1 small **hot red chilli**, halved
  and deseeded
4 **clementines**
2 **peaches**
½ **cantaloupe melon**,
  deseeded
75 g (3 oz) **blueberries**

Use the tip of a small, sharp knife to score the vanilla pod lengthways through to the centre. Put the measurement water and sugar in a saucepan and heat gently until the sugar has dissolved. Add the vanilla pod and chilli and heat gently for a further 2 minutes. Remove the pan from the heat and leave to cool while you prepare the fruit.

Remove the peel from the clementines and slice the flesh. Stone and slice the peaches. Cut the melon flesh into small chunks, removing and discarding the skin.

Put the prepared fruit and blueberries into a serving dish and mix together, then pour over the warm syrup, Serve immediately decorated with the chilli and half a vanilla pod (discard just before eating), or cover and chill until ready to serve.

For classic Italian fruit salad, mix together 500 ml (17 fl oz) good-quality, freshly squeezed orange juice and the grated rind of 1 lemon in a large bowl. Halve, stone and slice 2 peaches, peel, core and slice 1 pear and deseed and slice ½ small melon, discarding the skin, and add to the bowl with 150 g (5 oz) halved seedless red grapes. Stir in 3 tablespoons cherry liqueur and 3 tablespoons caster sugar, then chill until ready to serve.

banana lassi

Serves **4**
Preparation time **10 minutes**

3 ripe **bananas**, roughly
   chopped
500 g (17 oz) **natural yogurt**
250 ml (8 fl oz) **cold water**
1–2 tablespoons **caster sugar**
¼ teaspoon ground
   cardamom seeds, plus extra
   for decorating (optional)

Put all the ingredients in a food processor or blender and blend until smooth.

Pour into tall glasses and serve chilled, decorated with extra cardamom seeds if liked. This makes an ideal breakfast drink.

For a summer berry lassi, use only 1 banana, replace the cold water with 250 ml (8 fl oz) apple juice, omit the cardamom and add 200 g (7 oz) raspberries and 200 g (7 oz) blackberries.

affogato al caffe

Serves **4**
Preparation time **10 minutes**

8 scoops of **low-fat vanilla
  ice cream**
4 freshly made **espresso
  coffees**

Put 2 scoops of ice cream in each of 4 cappuccino cups or dessert bowls.

Pour a freshly made espresso coffee over each cup or bowl and serve immediately with biscotti, if liked.

For affogato al mocha, replace the vanilla ice cream with 8 scoops of rich, dark chocolate ice cream, pour over the coffee as above and top with 50 g (2 oz) finely chopped plain dark chocolate.

index

acknowledgements

Executive editor: Eleanor Maxfield
Text editor: Jo Murray
Art direction and design: Penny Stock
Photographer: Stephen Conroy
Home economist: Sara Lewis
Stylist: Liz Hippisley
Production: Caroline Alberti

Photography copyright © Octopus Publishing Group
Limited/Stephen Conroy, except the following: copyright
© Octopus Publishing Group/Will Heap 11 bottom,
14, 119, 133, 202, 221, 225; /Sandra Lane 53; /
William Lingwood 189; /David Munns 51, 69, 78, 100,
125; /Lis Parsons 9 top, 10 bottom, 16, 57, 59, 61, 75,
83, 87, 93, 169, 172, 179, 187, 197; /Gareth Sambidge
159, 213; /William Shaw 15 bottom; /Ian Wallace 8, 15
top, 27, 29, 33, 39, 41, 95, 137, 161, 181.